SPECTRUM®

Phonics

Grade 3

Spectrum®

An imprint of Carson-Dellosa Publishing LLC
Greensboro, North Carolina

Spectrum®
An imprint of Carson-Dellosa Publishing LLC
P.O. Box 35665
Greensboro, NC 27425 USA

Printed in the USA • All rights reserved. ISBN 0-7696-8293-6

07-063137811

Table of Contents Grade 3

Chapter 1 Phonics

Table of Contents, continued

Chapter 2 Word Structure

Table of Contents, continued

Lesson 1.1 Beginning Consonants

Look at the pictures below. On the line, write the first letter of the word that names each picture.

____iger   ____eaf   ____ike

____indow   ____urse   ____ear

Read the clues below. Circle the word that matches each clue.

1. I blow air to keep people cool in the summer. What am I?

    can   fan   pan

2. I am fun to read. I can tell a great story. What am I?

    book   hook   look

3. I live in oceans and lakes. Some people keep me as a pet. What am I?

    dish   fish   wish

4. I am a sweet birthday treat. Don't forget to blow out my candles!
   What am I?

    rake   bake   cake

5. You will find me at the beach. I can be hot to walk on. What am I?

    sand   hand   band

6. I come to your house every day. Sometimes, I travel a long way.
   What am I?

    mail   rail   sail

Lesson 1.1 Beginning Consonants

Look at the pictures below. Circle the letter that stands for the first sound you hear in each picture name.

m   n   b   b   d   t   s   v   z

p   l   h   v   w   r   f   b   h

Read each sentence below. Then, read the pair of words that follow. On the line, write the word that best completes each sentence.

1. Sam's family has three _____. (dogs, logs)

2. It is Sam's job to _____ them after school. (talk, walk)

3. Sometimes, he takes them to the _____. (park, dark)

4. They _____ to swim in the pond and bark at the squirrels. (dove, love)

5. When Sam whistles, his dogs know it is _____ to go home. (time, dime)

6. When they are _____, Sam gives each one a treat. (wood, good)

Lesson 1.2 Ending Consonants

Look at the pictures below. On the line, write the last letter of the word that names each picture.

_____   _____   _____

_____   _____   _____

Read each word below. Change the last letter of the word to make a new word. Write the new word on the line. It should rhyme with the three words below it.

1. car _____
      pat   flat   sat

2. skim _____
      trip   rip   sip

3. bus _____
      rug   shrug   tug

4. web _____
      forget   set   jet

5. sat _____
      tag   bag   flag

6. shot _____
      hop   drop   cop

7. hit _____
      slid   rid   lid

8. cob _____
      rot   hot   trot

Lesson 1.2 Ending Consonants

> When a word ends in a double letter, say the letter's sound only once.
>
> ki**ss**　　　do**ll**　　　cli**ff**　　　fi**zz**

Read the sentences below. Some words are not complete. Add **ss**, **ll**, **ff**, or **zz** to form the word or words that best complete each sentence.

1. The Rileys' goats eat the gra_____ in their yard.

2. Mr. Riley calls them the "Three Billy Goats Gru_____."

3. Maggy Riley brought in one of the goats for show-and-te_____.

4. Her teacher thought the goat might sme_____ or make a me_____.

5. "He might sni_____ our stu_____," said Maggy. "But he won't make a me_____."

6. The goat tried to eat a piece of fu_____, a do_____, and a bow on a girl's dre_____.

7. "No more animals in cla_____," Maggy's teacher said.

Read each set of words. Circle the word that names each picture.

rat	cut	pin
rag	cup	pill
ran	cub	pig
rap	cuff	pit

Lesson 1.3 Hard and Soft c and g

The letter **c** can make a hard sound, as in car and across. When **c** is followed by **e, i,** or **y,** it can make a soft sound, as in city and fancy.

The letter **g** can also make a hard sound, as in gas and ago. When **g** is followed by **e, i,** or **y,** it can make a soft sound, as in gentle and age.

Read the pairs of words below. Write **HC** on the line if they have a hard **c** sound. Write **SC** if they have a soft **c** sound.

1. _____ contest cabin

2. _____ rice pencil

3. _____ dancing cent

4. _____ second creek

5. _____ price center

6. _____ crab cute

Read the pairs of words below. Write **HG** on the line if they have a hard **g** sound. Write **SG** if they have a soft **g** sound.

1. _____ giraffe orange

2. _____ goldfish garden

3. _____ gem village

4. _____ signal frog

5. _____ gate dragon

6. _____ germ judge

Lesson 1.3 Hard and Soft **c** and **g**

Read the grocery list below. Circle the words that have a hard **c** or **g** sound. Underline the words that have a soft **c** or **g** sound.

Grocery List

grapes	celery	flour
cereal	clams	ice cream
carrots	oranges	sugar
gingerbread	milk	sliced bread
apples	lettuce	eggs
turkey	peanut butter	cat food

Look at each pair of pictures. Draw a line to match the hard or soft sound to each picture.

1.
soft **g**   hard **g**

2.
hard **c**   soft **c**

3.
hard **c**   soft **g**

4.
soft **c**   hard **g**

Lesson 1.3 Hard and Soft c and g

Read the paragraphs below. Look for words with the hard and soft **c** and **g** sounds. Then, write the words in the correct columns. You do not need to list the same word more than once. Hint: One word has both a hard and a soft **c** sound. List it in both columns.

Do you know anyone who collects marbles? Marbles are usually made of clay, glass, or plastic. Most marbles are about the size of a grape. There are a few huge marbles in museums. These giant marbles are about 12 feet tall!

People in many countries play games with marbles. In one game, the players draw a circle in the sand and place their marbles in the circle. They take turns using their marbles to push the other players' marbles out of the circle.

Some marbles are worth a lot of money. The price of a marble has to do with its color, age, and size. If you want to become a collector, join a club or read books to learn which ones are most valuable.

Hard c	Soft c	Hard g	Soft g
_____	_____	_____	_____
_____	_____	_____	_____
_____	_____	_____	_____
_____			
_____			
_____			
_____			
_____			

Lesson 1.3 Hard and Soft c and g

Read the clues below. On the line, write the word that matches each clue. Make sure that the word has the correct hard or soft **c** or **g** sound.

1. I live near ponds or creeks. I am green. I make a noise that sounds like ribbit. (hard **g**) _____

2. I come between first and third. I start with the letter **s**. (hard **c**) _____

3. I am a tool that is used for writing or drawing. I can be erased. I come in many colors. (soft **c**) _____

4. People use me when they bake sweet things. I can be brown or white. Some people sprinkle me on cereal or oatmeal. (hard **g**) _____

5. I am very cold. You can find me in the freezer. I am usually a cube. (soft **c**) _____

6. I live on a farm. I make milk. I make the sound moo. (hard **c**) _____

7. I am a bright color. I am also the name of a juicy fruit. I am the color of pumpkins. (soft **g**) _____

8. I come in a box. Lots of people eat me for breakfast. Usually, I am crunchy. (soft **c**) _____

Review Beginning and Ending Consonants

Look at each picture below. Say its name to yourself. Then, write the missing letter on the line.

ha_____   _____anana   _____angaroo

gra_____   _____ool   she_____

Read each sentence below. Then, read the word beside it. Replace the bold letter to form a word that makes sense in the sentence. Write it on the line.

1. The puffin is a bird that lives _____ the sea. (**f**ear)

2. It has black and white feathers, but its _____ and legs are orange. (bea**d**)

3. The puffin uses its strong _____ to help it swim underwater. (**r**ings)

4. Puffins can _____ several fish in their bills at one time. (**c**old)

5. These seabirds _____ live to be about 25 years old. (ca**p**)

6. Puffins can fly very _____ —about 50 miles per hour. (**l**ast)

7. Some people think puffins _____ a little like penguins. (**b**ook)

Review Hard and Soft c and g

Say each word to yourself. If it has a hard sound (like car or gas), circle hard. If it has a soft sound, like city or gentle, circle soft.

1. **garden**	hard	soft	5. **danger**	hard	soft
2. **gym**	hard	soft	6. **slice**	hard	soft
3. **attic**	hard	soft	7. **egg**	hard	soft
4. **case**	hard	soft	8. **edge**	hard	soft

Read each bold word below. Decide whether it has a hard or soft sound. Then, circle the word beside it that has the same sound.

1. **guppy**	gem	goat	age
2. **contest**	price	cuddle	decide
3. **cent**	ceiling	card	carrot
4. **guitar**	judge	geese	change
5. **general**	give	began	edge
6. **across**	coat	cent	prince
7. **dragon**	huge	gust	Georgia
8. **face**	traffic	cider	cry
9. **giant**	dog	gown	gel
10. **claw**	crisp	mice	bounce

Lesson 1.4 Beginning Two-Letter Blends with s

Some words begin with two consonants. When the sounds of the consonants are blended together, the two letters are called a **blend**.

Some blends are made with **s** plus another consonant. Each of the words below has an **s** blend.

scare   **sk**ate   **sm**ooth   **sn**icker   **sp**ell   **st**amp   **sw**eat

Say each picture name to yourself. Write the name of the picture on the line. Then, circle the **s** blend.

Read the sentences below. On each line, write an **s** blend from the pair in parentheses ( ). The word you form should make sense in the sentence.

1. Saturday afternoon was cold and _____owy. (sp, sn)

2. Carson and Samir decided to go _____ating on the frozen pond. (sk, sc)

3. Each boy wore a heavy jacket, a _____arf, and mittens. (sc, sw)

4. Carson and Samir _____ent all afternoon at the pond. (sn, sp)

5. They even _____arted a game of hockey with a few friends. (st, sk)

6. Samir was careful not to _____ill the cocoa as he poured it from the thermos. (sc, sp)

7. The cocoa was _____eet and hot. It was a great way to end a busy day. (sm, sw)

Lesson 1.4 Beginning Two-Letter Blends with s

Underline the **s** blend in each word below. Then, draw a line to match each word with another word that begins with the same **s** blend.

1. scar   snarl

2. skunk   spy

3. smear   skirt

4. sneeze   stiff

5. spaceship   swamp

6. stare   scout

7. sweep   smack

Read the paragraphs below. On each line, write a word from the box that has an **s** blend. The words you choose should make sense in the sentences. You will use one word twice.

| sky | smoke | skills | sniff | special | spark | stop | swiftly |

Wildfires can be very dangerous. It is the job of firefighters to

_____ the fires from spreading. They wear _____

gear to protect them from _____. These brave men and

women work hard to keep the fires under control. They _____

the air and scan the _____ above the forest for signs of

_____. They must act _____. Even a single

_____ from a campfire can start a wildfire. If the fire becomes

very large, as many as 10,000 firefighters might have to work together!

Fighting a wildfire is hard, hot, and dangerous. But most firefighters love

their jobs. They like the excitement, and they know that their

_____ can save people's lives.

Lesson 1.5 Beginning Two-Letter Blends with **l**

Some blends are made with **l** plus another consonant. Each of the words below has an **l** blend.

blank   **cl**ap   **fl**ash   **gl**ad   **pl**ace   **sl**eep

Say each picture name to yourself. Write the name of the picture on the line. Then, circle the **l** blend.

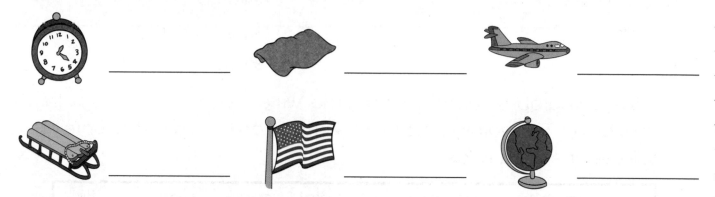

Read each meaning below. Choose a word from the box that matches the meaning. Write the word on the line.

closet	slow	cloud	flea	blackboard	planets	glue

1. _____ Mars, Jupiter, and Saturn are examples of this

2. _____ the opposite of quick

3. _____ a tiny insect that bites cats and dogs

4. _____ a white liquid used to stick two things together

5. _____ a puffy, white form in the sky

6. _____ a teacher uses chalk to write on this in a classroom

7. _____ a small room in which you keep your clothes

Lesson 1.5 Beginning Two-Letter Blends with l

Read the bold words below. Add **b, c, f, g, p,** or **s** to the beginning of each word to form as many new words as you can. Write the **l** blend words you formed on the lines.

lock	**lip**	**low**
_____ _____	_____ _____	_____ _____
_____	_____ _____	_____ _____
		_____

Read the sentences below. Circle the word with an **l** blend in each sentence. Then, think of another word that starts with the same blend. Write it on the line.

1. Jessy, Lena, and Cesar have a clubhouse in Lena's backyard. _____

2. The three friends were glad when Lena's dad said he'd help them build it. _____

3. The house is blue with a yellow door and yellow shutters. _____

4. A cheerful striped rug covers the wooden floor inside. _____

5. Jessy and Cesar made a special flag that hangs outside the front door. _____

6. Jessy climbed to the top of a stepladder to hang it. _____

7. On Saturday nights, their parents let them sleep in the little house. _____

8. The member made a secret pledge. _____

Lesson 1.6 Beginning Two-Letter Blends with r

> Some blends are made with **r** plus another consonant. Each of the words below has an **r** blend.
>
> **br**ake   **cr**aft   **dr**eam   **fr**ee   **gr**een   **pr**ess   **tr**ick

Read the paragraphs below. Circle the 12 words that begin with an **r** blend.

The California Gold Rush began in 1848. A man found a nugget of gold in a river. His find drew thousands of people to Gold Country. They came from all over the world to try their luck.

Many people dreamed of growing rich. All they needed was a shovel and a large pan. Miners dug up gravel from creeks, lakes, and rivers. They shook their pans and hoped to see a bit of bright, shiny gold at the bottom. Some riverbeds were rich with gold. A lucky miner might make 1,000 dollars in one day. Other miners worked for weeks without a profit. Would you have traveled across the country for the promise of gold?

Read the sentences below. On each line, write an **r** blend from the pair in parentheses ( ). The word you form should make sense in the sentence.

1. A nickname for the _____owds moving west was "49ers" because many left home in 1849. (fr, cr)

2. On the _____ail to California, water was hard to get. (tr, pr)

3. Some people _____ossing the desert paid 100 dollars for a cup of water! (fr, cr)

4. There was _____eat excitement each time someone struck it rich. (gr, dr)

5. Mining companies _____illed deep tunnels in the hills to search for gold. (dr, gr)

6. Today, you can pan for shiny _____ains of gold at parks all over the country. (gr, tr)

ew Two-Letter Blends

at the pictures and read the words. Circle the word that names each
e.

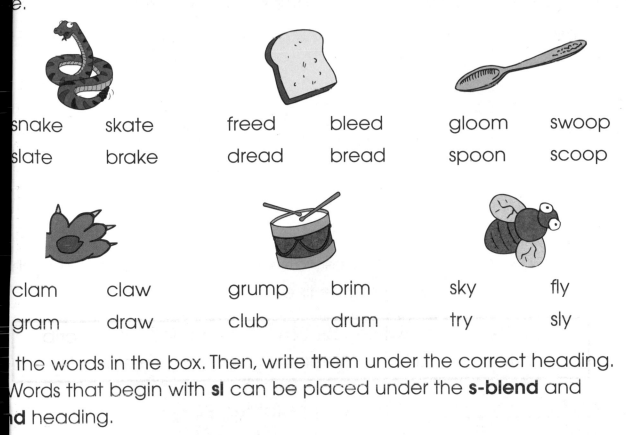

snake   skate   freed   bleed   gloom   swoop
slate   brake   dread   bread   spoon   scoop

clam   claw   grump   brim   sky   fly
gram   draw   club   drum   try   sly

the words in the box. Then, write them under the correct heading.
Words that begin with **sl** can be placed under the **s-blend** and
d heading.

plum	fruit	pretty	snail	trunk	smoky	scooter	slime
cry	slipper	drop	blaze	floppy	bring	skunk	glass

s blend   **l** blend   **r** blend

_____   _____   _____

_____   _____   _____

_____   _____   _____

_____   _____   _____

_____   _____   _____

_____   _____   _____

Lesson 1.6 Beginning Two-Letter Blends w

Revi

Underline the **r** blend in each word below. Then, draw a li
each word with another word that begins with the same

1. graze   brain
2. frost   truth
3. brave   droop
4. crow   grade
5. tractor   craft
6. drain   practice
7. pretzel   Friday

Read each meaning below. Choose a word from the box
the meaning. Write the word on the line.

principal	crawl	broom	grandfather	
price	trash	green	friend	brea

1. _____ your mother's father

2. _____ the amount something costs

3. _____ the color of grass

4. _____ a pal or buddy

5. _____ something you use to sweep the f

6. _____ a baby's bed

7. _____ the first meal you eat every day

8. _____ the head of a school

9. _____ garbage

10. _____ to move around on your hands an

Look
pictur

Read
Hint:
l-ble

Review Two-Letter Blends

Read the tongue twisters below. One blend is used several times in each tongue twister. Find the blend and circle it each time it is used. Then, think of another word that begins with that blend, and write it on the line.

1. Blackbirds like blueberries better than bluebirds like blackberries.
   _____

2. Mrs. Clump's class clapped when the clumsy clown climbed the cliff.
   _____

3. The French frog is friends with five fellows named Frank.
   _____

4. The skillful skunk knows how to ski, skate, skip, sketch, and skateboard.
   _____

5. The cricket and the crane crunched crispy crackers by the creek.
   _____

6. The speedy spider spun a sparkly web in space. _____

7. The train traveled through traffic with a troop of trucks and tractors.
   _____

Now, choose a beginning blend and write a tongue twister of your own.

_____

_____

_____

_____

_____

Lesson 1.7 Beginning Three-Letter Blends

Some words begin with three consonants. Blend the sounds of the consonants together when you say the words. Each of the words below starts with a three-letter blend.

scrape   **spl**it   **spr**ing   **str**ipe

Read each word in bold. Circle the three-letter blend. Then, underline the word beside it that has the same blend.

1. **screen**   strike   scream   scold
2. **straight**   stray   sprout   splinter
3. **spray**   strong   scrape   spring
4. **split**   spine   splash   streak
5. **stream**   scratch   straw   sprain
6. **scrub**   scrap   scoop   strain

Read the paragraphs below. On each line, write a three-letter blend from the box. The word you form should make sense in the sentence.

scr	spl	spr	str

Addison and Luke Wallace found a _____ay cat in their yard. She had gray and white _____ipes and pretty green eyes. Mrs. Wallace helped them _____ub some old cat food dishes so they could feed her.

"She looks friendly," said Mrs. Wallace, "but she is still a _____ange cat. I want you both to be careful not to get _____atched."

The Wallaces made a cozy bed out of some fresh _____aw from the barn. They _____ead an old blanket over the straw. When Luke gave the cat some milk, she _____ashed in it with her paw. Then she licked the milk off her paw. Finally, she _____etched, curled up in a ball, and went to sleep.

Addison laughed. "I guess she feels right at home here!"

Lesson 1.7 Beginning Three-Letter Blends

Look at each picture and the word below it. The word that names the picture will begin with a three-letter blend (**scr**, **spl**, **str**, or **spr**). It will rhyme with the word in bold. Write the word on the line.

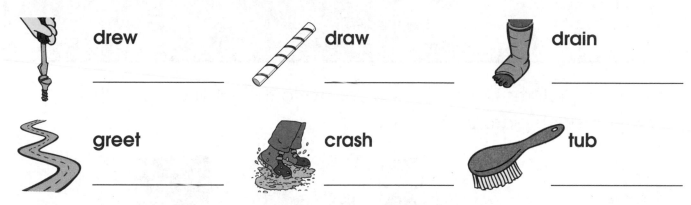

drew
_____

draw
_____

drain
_____

greet
_____

crash
_____

tub
_____

Read the clues below. On the line, write the word that matches each clue. The number of letters in each word is in parentheses ( ) at the end of the sentence. Remember, each word will start with one of these three-letter blends: **scr**, **spl**, **str**, or **spr**.

1. I'm used to water a lawn. Kids like to run through me on a hot day. (9 letters) _____

2. I am the season that comes between winter and summer. (6 letters) _____

3. I am another word for yell. (6 letters) _____

4. I am a sweet summer fruit. I am a red berry with tiny seeds and a green stem. Some people make jam out of me. (10 letters) _____

5. I am what you do when you have an itch. (7 letters) _____

6. I am powerful. I am a word that means the opposite of weak. (6 letters) _____

7. I am another word for road. Cars drive on me. (6 letters) _____

Lesson 1.8 Ending Blends

Some blends come at the ends of words. Blend the two consonants together when you say the words. Each of the words below has an ending blend.

craft   melt   ramp   drink   bent

Look at the pictures below. On the Line, write the ending blend that completes each picture's name.

pai_____

la_____

qui_____

chipmu_____

gi_____

ju_____

Read the sentences below. Circle the ending blends (**ft, lt, mp, nk, nt**) you find in each sentence.

1. Mr. Flores is a scientist who works with a chimp named Moe.

2. Mr. Flores is trying to learn how animals think.

3. Moe cannot talk, but Mr. Flores spent a long time teaching him sign language.

4. Whenever Mr. Flores felt that Moe earned a reward, he gave him a plump banana.

5. Moe learned to make signs for words like drink, soft, sleep, want, and funny.

6. When Moe signs a word correctly, he jumps for joy.

7. "You're a champ, Moe," cheers Mr. Flores.

Lesson 1.8 Ending Blends

Read each sentence and the set of words that follows it. Choose the word that best completes the sentence and write it on the line. Then, circle the ending blend.

1. Next weekend, we are going to _____ at the Blue Spruce State Park. (camp, damp, colt)

2. We'll sleep in our new, three-room _____. (rent, tank, tent)

3. Dad said that we'll set up camp on a bed of _____ pine needles. (sift, soft, salt)

4. I can't wait to _____ down Spruce River. (raft, rank, craft)

5. My sister, Linh, is worried the raft will _____. (wink, sent, sink)

6. My uncle _____ us some lifejackets, so now Linh is excited too. (lent, tint, lamp)

7. At night, we'll _____ cocoa and roast marshmallows. (dunk, drink, drift)

8. I like my marshmallows _____ to a crisp on the outside. (bent, shift, burnt)

9. Last night, I _____ so excited I could hardly sleep. (felt, front, blink)

10. I just hope we don't get sprayed by a _____ like my grandpa did the last time he went camping! (slump, skunk, trunk)

Lesson 1.9 More Ending Blends

Some blends come at the ends of words. Blend the two consonants together when you say the words. Each of the words below has an ending blend.

child   ba**nd**   de**sk**   be**st**

On the line, write the ending blend (**ld, nd, sk, st**) that completes each picture's name.

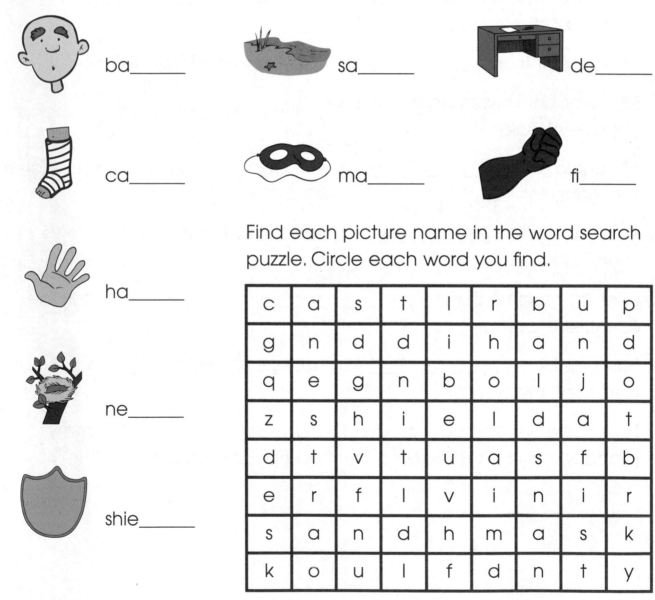

ba_____   sa_____   de_____

ca_____   ma_____   fi_____

ha_____

Find each picture name in the word search puzzle. Circle each word you find.

ne_____

shie_____

c	a	s	t	l	r	b	u	p
g	n	d	d	i	h	a	n	d
q	e	g	n	b	o	l	j	o
z	s	h	i	e	l	d	a	t
d	t	v	t	u	a	s	f	b
e	r	f	l	v	i	n	i	r
s	a	n	d	h	m	a	s	k
k	o	u	l	f	d	n	t	y

Lesson 1.9 More Ending Blends

Read each word in bold. Circle the ending blend. Then, underline the word beside it that has the same blend.

1. **wrist**	risk	roast	wild
2. **dusk**	build	send	ask
3. **mold**	field	blind	sound
4. **stand**	child	grind	post
5. **just**	task	east	sold
6. **unfold**	held	hound	twist
7. **wand**	trust	disk	and
8. **task**	ask	wind	billfold

Read each meaning below. Choose a word from the box that matches the meaning. Write the word on the line.

blend	cold	mask	band	dentist	toast	old	west	gold	disk

1. _____ a doctor who takes care of your teeth

2. _____ the direction that is the opposite of east

3. _____ something you put over your face as a costume

4. _____ a group of people who make music together

5. _____ to mix together

6. _____ the opposite of young

7. _____ a very valuable yellow metal

8. _____ a shiny, round piece of plastic used to store music or computer files

9. _____ chilly; not warm

10. _____ slices of lightly cooked bread

Review Three Letter Blends and Ending Blends

Look at each picture below. On the first line, write the word that names the picture. Circle the ending blend. Now, choose a word from the box that has the same ending blend. Write it on the second line.

REVIEW: CHAPTER 1 LESSONS 7-9

left	crust	amount	salt	honk	dump

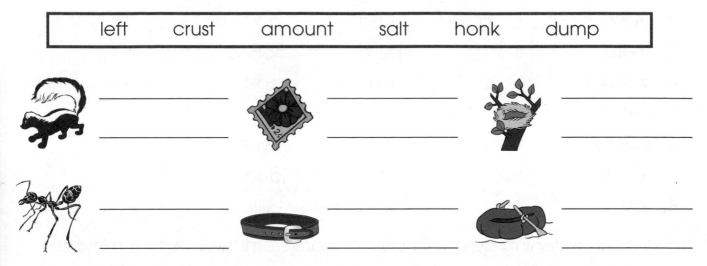

Read the story below. Find the 14 words that begin with a three-letter blend (**scr**, **spl**, **spr**, **str**). Circle each word you find.

On Saturday night, we had strawberry shortcake for dessert. I split a big piece with my brother, Drew. The whole family sat outside on the screened porch. We watched people stroll down the street. All of a sudden, we heard something strange. There was a low, buzzing sound all around us. My brother sprang out of his chair, and his shortcake splattered on the ground.

"Mosquitoes!" screamed Drew, as he sprinted inside. Dozens of mosquitoes streamed in through a small tear in one of the screens. I started to scratch just looking at them.

"Everyone inside," said Mom. She scraped up the shortcake from the ground. "I guess we found out what mosquitoes like best for dessert," she said with a laugh.

Review Three Letter Blends and Ending Blends

Read the paragraphs below. The words in bold are not complete. Complete the words by choosing an ending blend from the pair in parentheses ( ) and writing it on the line. The words you form should make sense in the sentences.

Every autumn, you probably see hundreds of acorns on the **grou**_____ (nd, ld). Acorns are the fruit of oak trees. **Wi**_____ (mp, ld) animals, like birds, squirrels, bears, **a**_____ (sk, nd) deer, eat these little nuts. But did you ever **thi**_____ (nk, nt) that people could eat acorns too? Native Americans used acorns in many ways. They could **gri**_____ (ld, nd) the nuts to make acorn flour, or they could boil and **roa**_____ (st, sk) them. **Mo**_____ (lt, st) acorns are bitter, so they are not eaten raw.

If you **wa**_____ (nt, nd) to prepare acorns at home, collect some **rou**_____ (nd, mp), **plu**_____ (st, mp) acorns. They should not be **so**_____ (lt, ft) or have any holes or cracks. Use a nutcracker to get the nut out of the shell. Put the nuts in a pot with water **a**_____ (nd, st) boil them. When the water turns **almo**_____ (st, ft) brown, change it. Keep doing this until the water doesn't change color. Then, bake the acorns at a low heat for about two hours. You can sprinkle **sa**_____ (lt, nk) on them **a**_____ (mp, nd) eat them for a tasty snack.

Lesson 1.10 Beginning Digraphs

A **digraph** is a combination of two letters that stand for one sound. You do not hear the sound of each letter in a digraph. Instead, the letters form a new sound.

- The digraph **sh** makes the sound you hear in **sh**eet, **sh**op, and **sh**y.
- The digraph **ch** makes the sound you hear in **ch**ild, **ch**in, and **ch**eckers.

Look at each picture below. On the first line, write the word that names the picture. Circle the digraph. Now, think of another word that has the same digraph. Write it on the second line.

Read the clues below. On the line, write the word that matches each clue. Remember, each word will start with a digraph.

1. I am the opposite of dull. You need to be careful with me so you don't get cut. _____

2. I am an animal that lives in the ocean. I have a large fin on my back. Many people are afraid of me. _____

3. I am the opposite of expensive. _____

4. I am part of your face. You can find me below your mouth. _____

Lesson 1.10 Beginning Digraphs

Read the words below. One word in each set does not belong. Underline the digraph of the word that does not belong in the set.

1. shallow   child   shave
2. shine   charm   chime
3. shin   shot   chip
4. shawl   shelf   choose
5. cherry   shower   chilly
6. shade   checker   chant

Read the sentences below. Complete each incomplete word with the digraph **sh** or **ch**.

1. Devon loves to bake _____ocolate _____ip cookies with his grandma.

2. After school, Diana and her mom will go _____opping for new

   _____oes.

3. Please don't _____ange the _____annel until there is an ad.

4. "Did you see the _____ark?" _____outed Bridget.

5. _____ould we _____ovel the snow this afternoon?

6. Maria never _____eats when she plays _____ess.

7. I need to find the _____ampoo before I take a _____ower.

8. The baker made three _____erry _____eesecakes.

9. Would you like _____eese on your _____icken sandwich?

10. Deepak _____owed Leo how to float in the _____allow end of the pool.

Lesson 1.12 Ending Digraphs

Some digraphs, like **sh**, **ch**, **th**, and **ph** can also come at the ends of words.

pu**sh**   bea**ch**   wi**th**   gra**ph**

Read each meaning below. Choose the word from the box that matches the meaning. Write the word on the line.

lunch   teeth   brush   watch   match   north   leash   photograph

1. _____ a small clock you wear on your wrist

2. _____ what you do every day to your teeth and your hair

3. _____ a picture taken with a camera

4. _____ the meal between breakfast and dinner

5. _____ the opposite of south

6. _____ a long cord or strap used when walking a dog

7. _____ something used to light a candle or start a fire

8. _____ the white things in your mouth used for chewing

Read the sentences below. One ending digraph is used several times in each sentence. Find the digraph and circle it each time it is used. Then, think of another word that ends with that digraph and write it in the blank.

1. _____ Each of the kids ate a sandwich and a peach for lunch.

2. _____ I wish you would wash that dish before you mash the potatoes.

3. _____ Both of the Cohen boys are in the fifth grade and love math and hockey.

Lesson 1.12 Ending Digraphs

On the line, write the ending digraph that completes each picture's name.

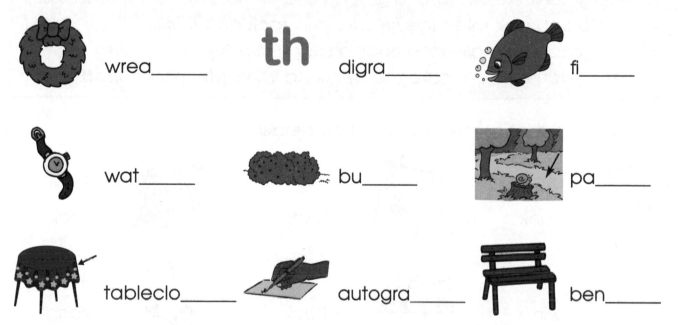

wrea_____   **th**   digra_____   fi_____

wat_____   bu_____   pa_____

tableclo_____   autogra_____   ben_____

Find each picture name in the word search puzzle. Circle the words you find.

t	a	b	l	e	c	l	o	t	h
k	u	u	r	e	n	t	l	p	u
o	t	s	v	j	b	a	c	a	n
w	o	h	h	f	d	n	s	t	n
q	g	r	t	i	z	f	q	h	b
x	r	y	t	s	y	s	p	a	e
w	a	t	c	h	o	s	r	d	n
i	p	u	w	r	e	a	t	h	c
l	h	f	d	i	g	r	a	p	h

Lesson 1.13 More Ending Digraphs

> Other digraphs, like **ck**, **ng**, and **gh**, can also come at the ends of words.
> - The digraph **ck** makes the /k/ sound in *sack* and *thick*.
> - The digraph **ng** makes the ending sound in *hang* and *young*.
> - The digraph **gh** can make the /f/ sound in *tough* and *enough*.

Circle the word that names each picture below.

duck
dunk

sink
swing

laugh
lock

wick
wing

tough
truck

sock
song

Read the sentences below. Some words are not complete. Add **ck**, **ng**, or **gh** to form the word or words that best complete each sentence.

1. Next week, Alex is goi_____ to compete in a spelling bee.

2. He has made it to the finals, so he knows the words will be tou_____.

3. Before he leaves, Alex wants to che_____ his backpa_____ for his dictionary and flashcards.

4. He doesn't want to spell a word wro_____ because he didn't study hard enou_____.

5. Alex is you_____, but he has been traini_____ for a lo_____ time.

6. Sometimes, learni_____ the meani_____ of a word can help Alex spell it.

7. As Alex spells his words, he hears the ti_____ of the clo_____ and hopes the buzzer doesn't ri_____.

Lesson 1.13 More Ending Digraphs

Read the paragraphs below. Complete the words by choosing a~ digraph from the pair in parentheses ( ) and writing it on the line. The words you form should make sense in the sentences.

Have you ever heard of a triathlon? It is a tou_____ (ck, gh) race of swimmi_____ (ng, ck), runni_____ (gh, ng), and biki_____ (ck, ng). The most famous race is called the Ironman Triathlon. It takes place in Hawaii. The athletes must swim more than 2 miles, bike 112 miles, and run 26 miles. Not all triathlons are this lo_____ (ng, gh). Even kids can compete in the Ironkids Triathlon.

Traini_____ (gh, ng) for a race can be harder than people expect. A little bit of lu_____ (ck, ng) isn't enou_____ (ck, gh). The athletes spend lots of time at the tra_____ (ng, ck), in the pool, and on bike trails. They are always racing against the clo_____ (ck, gh). Some belo_____ (gh, ng) to clubs. Others choose to blo_____ (ng, ck) everythi_____ (ng, ck) out and work on their own.

One thing is for sure: After finishi_____ (ng, ck) a race, the athletes know they can do anythi_____ (gh, ng)!

Now, write the words you completed on the lines beside the correct headings.

ck: _____ _____ _____ _____

ng: _____ _____ _____ _____ _____

_____ _____ _____ _____

gh: _____ _____

Lesson 1.14 Silent Consonants

In some consonant pairs, one letter is silent.
- The letters **kn** can make the /n/ sound you hear in **kn**ot and **kn**ee. The **k** is silent.
- The letters **wr** can make the /r/ sound you hear in **wr**ap and **wr**ong. The **w** is silent.
- The letters **sc** can make the /s/ sound you hear iin **sc**ience and **sc**ene. The **c** Is silent.

Look at each picture, and read the word beside it. Change the letter or letters in bold to **kn**, **wr**, or **sc** so that the word names the picture. Write the new word on the line.

 trot _____

 twinkle _____

 bright _____

Read each word in bold. Circle the word beside it that has the same beginning sound. If you are not sure, say the words out loud.
Hint: Two sounds can be the same even when the spellings are different.
(Example: knit and nice)

1. **knock**   kick   never   kid
2. **wrestle**   wrinkle   west   Wednesday
3. **science**   cute   scissors   shop
4. **knew**   wren   king   knob
5. **scene**   seven   scare   crumb
6. **wrist**   wild   wrapper   whisper
7. **knead**   nest   kiss   wreath
8. **wrote**   wire   knock   rail

Lesson 1.14 Silent Consonants

Read each sentence below. Then, read the pair of words that follow. On the line, write the word that best completes each sentence.

1. Amelia loves to read and hopes to be a _____ when she grows up. (writer, wrapper)

2. _____ the dough until it feels soft and stretchy. (Knit, Knead)

3. José's brother is on the _____ team. (wrestling, wrinkle)

4. I love the _____ of cinnamon and apples in the air when we bake a pie. (scent, science)

5. Carter _____ what time the bus will come. (kneel, knows)

6. Bakari's aunt is a _____ who works with dangerous materials. (scientist, scissors)

7. Grandma _____ me two sweaters for my birthday. (knew, knit)

8. The students in Ms. Hopple's class made autumn _____ out of dried leaves and branches. (wreaths, wrecks)

Read each meaning below. Choose a word from the box that matches the meaning. Write the word on the line.

knock	scent	wrong	wrap	scissors	knight

1. _____ not correct; the opposite of right

2. _____ a smell

3. _____ a soldier from long ago who fought wearing heavy armor

4. _____ two blades that are used for cutting; they come in pairs

5. _____ to cover a gift with colorful paper

Review Digraphs and Silent Consonants

Remember, a **digraph** is a combination of two letters that stand for one sound. Together, the letters form a new sound. Some digraphs come at the beginnings of words. Others come at the ends of words. **Sh**, **th**, **ck**, and **ng** are examples of digraphs.

ship   **th**imble   sti**ck**   si**ng**

Read each clue below. In the blank, write the word that matches the clue. Each word will begin or end with one of these digraphs: **sh, ch, th, wh, ph, ck, ng, gh**.

1. You hear me during a storm. I make loud booms and crashes in the

   sky. ____ ____ ____ ____ ____ ____ ____

2. I am the number that comes between twelve and fourteen.

   ____ ____ ____ ____ ____ ____ ____ ____

3. People eat me for lunch. I am made with two slices of bread and

   some filling. ____ ____ ____ ____ ____ ____ ____ ____

4. I am fluffy and white. Wool is made from my fur. I make this sound:

   baaaaa. ____ ____ ____ ____ ____

5. I wear a crown. A queen is my partner. ____ ____ ____ ____

6. I am a dark color. I am the opposite of white. ____ ____ ____ ____ ____

7. I am what a person does when something is funny.

   ____ ____ ____ ____ ____

8. You can use me to call people. When you have a call, I make a

   ringing noise. ____ ____ ____ ____ ____

Review Digraphs and Silent Consonants

Read the paragraphs below. Complete the words by choosing letters from the pair in parentheses ( ). The words you form should make sense in the sentences.

Benjamin Franklin was a printer, an inventor, a _____iter (kn, wr), and a _____ientist (sh, sc). When he was you_____ (th, ng), Franklin owned his own printing _____op (wh, sh). He printed newspapers and a popular book called Poor Richard's Almana_____ (ck, ng).

Ben Franklin loved books and helped set up the first public library in America. He was also known as one of the Foundi_____ (ng, ck) Fathers of our country. His autogra_____ (gh, ph) is on the Declaration of Independence and the Constitution. He fou_____t (gh, th) against things, like slavery, that he _____ew (kn, wr) were _____ong (wr, sc). Some people _____ink (sh, th) he was ahead of his time.

Franklin proved that li_____tning (gh, ph) is a form of electricity. Later, he invented the lightni_____ (ck, ng) rod. He also invented the wood stove, swim fins, and a new type of glasses that helped people with bad eyesi_____t (th, gh).

Franklin was an amazi_____ (ng, ck) person. _____at (Wh, Th) would you ask him if he were still alive today?

Did You Know? Some words change their spelling over time. Today, the word almanac ends with a **c**. In Ben Franklin's day, it was spelled with a **ck** (almanack). Do you know any old-fashioned spellings for other words?

Lesson 1.16 Short Vowels

The letter **i** can make the short vowel sound you hear in words like chimp and fill.

Look at each picture. Write the word that names the picture on the line. It will rhyme with the word in bold.

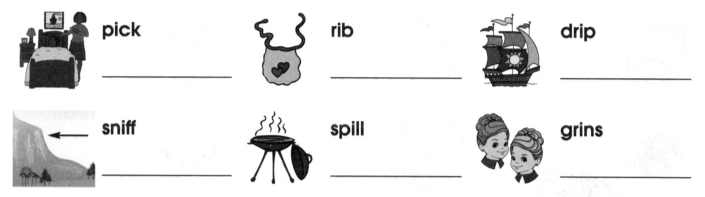

pick

_____

rib

_____

drip

_____

sniff

_____

spill

_____

grins

_____

Read the sentences below. On each line, write a word from the pair in parentheses ( ). The word you choose should make sense in the sentence.

1. _____ (Big, Bring) Ben is the name of a famous clock tower and bell in London.

2. The hour bell weighs almost 14 tons and fills the air with a loud

   _____ (limping, ringing) sound.

3. A team of 16 horses _____ (spilled, hitched) to a wagon pulled the bell to the tower in 1858.

4. The clock has been in many _____ (films, kicks).

5. The tower is _____ (thick, lit) up against London's night sky.

6. In October 2005, the hands of the clock were _____ (skid, still) for 33 hours.

7. Even with heavy _____ (wind, cliff), snow, and storms, the clock does not break down often.

Lesson 1.16 Short Vowels

The letter **o** can make the short vowel sound you hear in words like chop and dog.

Look at the pictures and read the words below. Circle the word that names each picture.

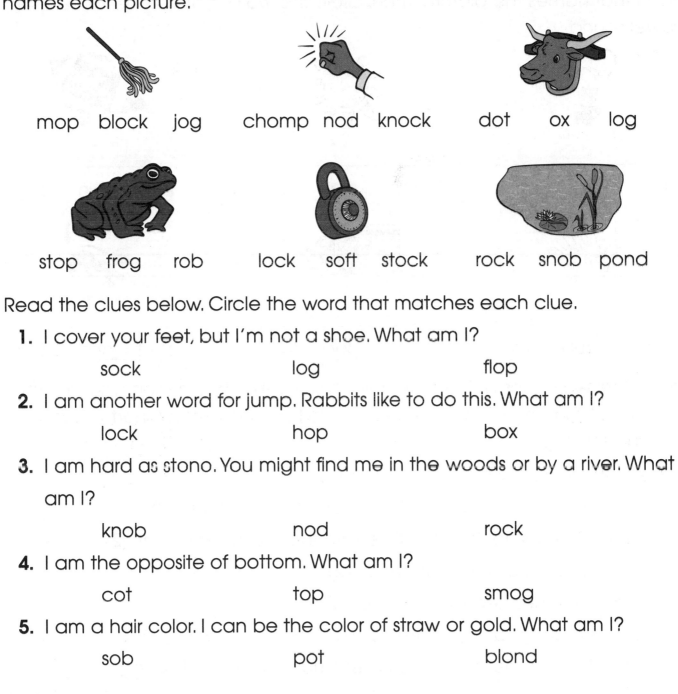

mop   block   jog   chomp   nod   knock   dot   ox   log

stop   frog   rob   lock   soft   stock   rock   snob   pond

Read the clues below. Circle the word that matches each clue.

1. I cover your feet, but I'm not a shoe. What am I?

   sock   log   flop

2. I am another word for jump. Rabbits like to do this. What am I?

   lock   hop   box

3. I am hard as stone. You might find me in the woods or by a river. What am I?

   knob   nod   rock

4. I am the opposite of bottom. What am I?

   cot   top   smog

5. I am a hair color. I can be the color of straw or gold. What am I?

   sob   pot   blond

Lesson 1.16 Short Vowels

The letter **u** can make the short vowel sound you hear in words like dug and plum.

Look at the pictures and read the words below. On the line, write the word that names the picture. Then, circle the word that has the same short vowel sound.

_____
fluff   Fred   think

_____
sat   lunch   left

_____
ham   thin   junk

_____
plot   scrub   kiss

_____
mud   job   hip

_____
dent   part   dust

Read the sentences below. Circle each word that has a short **u** sound. The number at the end of the sentence will tell you how many short **u** words you should find.

1. Dylan plays the drums in a band. (1)
2. Simon strums his guitar and hums along to the tune. (2)
3. Thalia thumps her hand in time with the drummer's beat. (2)
4. Pedro puffs into a shiny trumpet. (2)
5. Clara clutches her trusty clarinet. (2)
6. Chelsea chugs a cup of fruit punch and starts to sing. (3)
7. Shonda shuts the door, and Peter plugs in the speakers. (2)

Lesson 1.16 Short Vowels

Read the paragraphs below. Each of the words in bold has a short vowel sound. Listen to the vowel sound and write each word in bold under the correct heading. An example has been added below each heading to help you.

Have you ever heard of the author Eve Bunting? She **has** written more **than** 150 books for **kids**. She writes about many different **things** that are important to her in some way. Eve has written about animals, like **ducks** and **dogs**. She has written about mummies, the **Civil** War, and growing **up** in Ireland. She has even written a book about the great **ship** Titanic.

When Eve **visits** classes, students have **lots** of questions for her. Many of **them** want to know where she **gets** her ideas. Eve **tells** them that an idea might hit her anywhere. For example, she **got** the idea to write her **mummy** book after a **trip** to the museum.

Eve has said that she likes to write books **that** make children **ask** questions. If you think you might like to try an Eve Bunting book, **check** your library. It is sure to have many books by this popular writer.

short a	short e	short i	short o	short u
cap	pet	kick	stop	snug

Lesson 1.17 Long Vowel Sounds

The letter **a** can make a long sound, as in cake, when it is followed by a consonant and silent **e**. Sometimes, this pattern is called VCe. That stands for Vowel + Consonant + Silent **e**. The silent **e** makes the vowel say its name.

The words in bold all have the short **a** sound. Add silent **e** to each word and write the new word on the line. Then, draw a line to match each new word to a rhyming word in the second column.

1. **cap** + **e** = _____   sale

2. **sam** + **e** = _____   plane

3. **man** + **e** = _____   cage

4. **past** + **e** = _____   tape

5. **hat** + **e** = _____   came

6. **mad** + **e** = _____   fade

7. **pal** + **e** = _____   taste

8. **rag** + **e** = _____   rate

Read each word in bold below. Underline the world beside that has the same long vowel sound.

1. **shade**	sharp	wage	cast
2. **space**	lamp	call	quake
3. **whale**	vane	champ	saggy
4. **flake**	dark	past	vase
5. **blame**	band	cave	tax
6. **crate**	waste	splat	crack

Lesson 1.17 Long Vowel Sounds

> The letter **i** can make a long sound, as in hide, when it is followed by a consonant and silent **e**.

Read the silly sentences below. Circle each word that has the long **i** sound spelled **i-consonant-e**.

1. The little mice use a lot of spice when they make white rice.

2. If you dive at low tide, you can see creatures with spines, spikes, and stripes.

3. We will dine on a nice slice of lime that's ripe from the vine.

4. If you are wise, you will hike nine miles to see the sun rise.

5. The swine will glide and slide in the slime each time the weather is fine.

6. Wipe and shine each side of the shoes in the pile twice.

7. Let us fly five fine kites tied with twine.

8. The bride will glide for five miles while she skydives.

Read the long **i** words in the box. Write some silly sentences of your own. You can use other long **i** words if you like, but they should have the **i-consonant-e** spelling. You may use the words in the box more than once.

nice	crime	hide	ride	spike	stripe	white
write	hike	kite	mice	drive	five	nine

1. _____

2. _____

3. _____

4. _____

Lesson 1.17 Long Vowel Sounds

> • The letter **o** can make a long sound, as in rope, when it is followed by a consonant and silent **e**.
> • The letter **o** can also make a long sound when it is followed only by silent **e**, as in Joe.

Look at the pictures below. On the lines, write the words that name the pictures. Each picture name will have a long **o** sound.

Read the meanings below. On the lines, write the words from the box that match the meanings.

whole	home	doe	joke	mole	rose	Rome

1. _____ a female deer

2. _____ a small animal that lives underground

3. _____ a city in Italy

4. _____ something funny you tell other people

5. _____ another word for house

6. _____ a type of flower

7. _____ the opposite of half

Lesson 1.17 Long Vowel Sounds

> • The letter **u** can make a long sound, as in cute or rule, when it is followed by a consonant and silent **e**.
> • The letter **u** can also make a long sound when it is followed only by silent **e**, as in due.

Read each word in bold. Underline the word beside it that has the same long **u** sound. If you are not sure, say the words out loud.

1. **use**	dug	cube	cut
2. **tube**	tub	run	rude
3. **June**	plume	plum	truck
4. **glue**	jump	tune	thump
5. **rule**	dude	rug	hum
6. **fuse**	shut	cute	just
7. **mute**	must	fuse	much

Read the sentences below. On the line, write a long **u** word from the pair in parentheses ( ). The word you choose should make sense in the sentence.

1. Every _____ (June, cube), _____ (tune, Sue) prunes the lilac bushes in her yard.

2. One _____ (fume, rule) at the library is that you return books when they are _____ (sun, due).

3. Play me a pretty _____ (clue, tune) on your _____ (flute, dude).

4. Hannah's _____ (cute, cut), gray _____ (huge, mule) has long, soft ears.

5. Sayako found all the _____ (clues, dust), and now she's looking for the prize.

Lesson 1.17 Long Vowel Sounds

Look at each picture below. On the first line, write the word that names the picture. Then, think of another word that has the same long vowel sound. Write it on the second line.

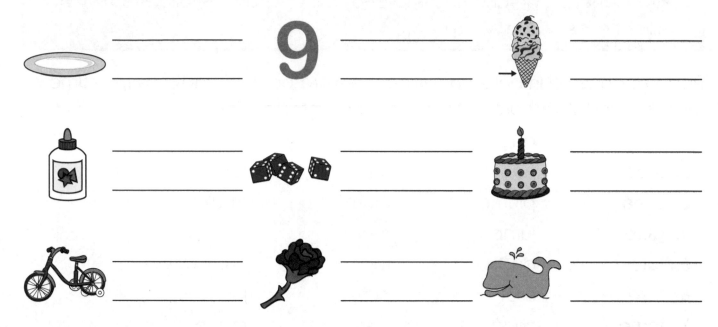

Find each picture name in the word search puzzle. Circle each word you find.

r	y	c	a	k	e	g	h	l	g
d	u	q	b	b	w	a	j	o	l
b	p	s	c	e	h	r	f	n	u
l	t	v	p	l	a	t	e	s	e
h	w	u	c	n	l	c	e	d	a
b	h	r	o	s	e	r	p	i	x
b	j	k	n	c	e	o	l	c	f
n	i	n	e	s	b	i	k	e	t
h	n	d	a	j	y	q	d	e	z

Lesson 1.17 Long Vowel Sounds

Read the paragraphs below. Each of the words in bold has a long vowel sound. Listen to the vowel sound and write each word in bold under the correct heading. An example has been added below each heading to help you.

Does your **state** have a nickname? The story of a state's nickname can be a **clue** to its history. It tells you what the people who live there think is important about their **home**.

Florida is called the Sunshine State because the sun **shines** there all year long. Kentucky is the Bluegrass State. Bluegrass is actually green, but the buds are **blue**. They can **make** fields of grass look blue. Maine is known as the **Pine** Tree State. It has more than 17 million acres of forest!

Maryland goes by the **name** Old **Line** State. Some people think George Washington named Maryland for its line troops during the Revolutionary War.

One of Michigan's names is the Great **Lake** State. Michigan is **close** to four of the Great Lakes. There are thousands of smaller lakes around the state too.

Texas is the **Lone** Star State. There are a few different ideas about how Texas got its name. One thing is for sure—a single star has been on the Texas flag since before it was even a state.

If you could **vote** on a new nickname for your state, what would it be?

long **a**	long **i**	long **o**	long **u**
take	ride	zone	due
_____	_____	_____	_____
_____	_____	_____	_____
_____	_____	_____	_____
_____	_____	_____	

Lesson 1.18 Vowel Sounds (ai, ay, ei)

> • The letters **ai** can make the long **a** sound you hear in m**ai**d
> and br**ai**n.
> • The letters **ay** can make the long **a** sound you hear in cl**ay**
> and spr**ay**.
> • The letters **ei** can make the long **a** sound you hear in w**ei**gh
> and sl**ei**gh.

Read the clues below. Underline the word that matches each clue.

1. People use me to catch fish, but I'm not a fishing pole. What am I?

   play   bait   sleigh

2. I am the sound a horse makes. What am I?

   vein   neigh   sway

3. There are 365 of me every year. I am 24 hours long. What am I?

   vase   pain   day

4. I am a state in the Northeast. I am known for lobster. It gets very cold
   here in the winter. What am I?

   stay   Maine   Spain

5. Brides often wear me. I am usually white, and I cover the bride's face.
   What am I?

   veil   rain   tray

6. I am a type of bird. I am usually blue. I have a loud voice. What am I?

   flame   jay   skate

7. I wear my house on my back. What am I?

   gray   cape   snail

8. I am the number that comes between seven and nine. What am I?

   eight   play   laid

Lesson 1.18 Vowel Sounds (**ai, ay, ei**)

Read the paragraphs below. On each line, write a word from the pair in parentheses ( ). The word you choose should make sense in the sentence.

A rail _____ (trail, hay) can be a great place to bike, walk, or ride horses. _____ (Veil, Rail) trails used to be _____ (train, wait) tracks. Trains were the best way to send _____ (mail, sleigh) and heavy _____ (freight, clay) across the country. Over time, people started using trucks more than trains. Lots of old tracks that were no longer being used _____ (swayed, remained). Cities and states _____ (paid, grain) for the land and the tracks. They wanted to turn these areas into greenspace.

The first rail trail opened in Wisconsin in 1965. Since then, thousands of other trails have been _____ (rain, laid) from _____ (Maine, plain) to California. The longest one is in Missouri. It stretches about 200 miles!

People like rail trails because they are usually _____ (weigh, straight) and flat. Since they used to be train tracks, they are often near cities. If you would like to visit a rail trail near your home, you _____ (braid, may) want to check out this Web site: www.trailink.com. You'll find a great place to get _____ (away, pay) for the _____ (rain, day). Grab your bike, a friend, or the _____ (tray, reins) of a horse, and have fun.

Lesson 1.19 Vowel Sounds (**ee**, **ea**, **ie**)

- The letters **ee** make the long **e** sound you hear in k**ee**p and gr**ee**n.
- The letters **ea** can make the long **e** sound you hear in b**ea**d.
- The letters **ie** can make the long **e** sound you hear in ch**ie**f.

Look at the pictures below. On the line, write the word that names each picture. Each picture name will have a long **e** sound.

Look at each picture below. Write the name of the picture next to it. Then, write each word from the box under the heading that has the same long **e** spelling.

treat	seed	reach	field	three	sea	collie	piece
sneeze	niece	beat	creek	chief	plead	speech	

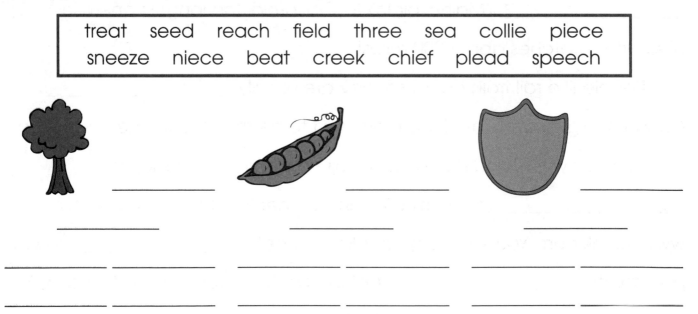

Lesson 1.19 Vowel Sounds (ee, ea, ie)

Read the sentences and the pairs of letters that follow. Write the correct long **e** spelling on the line.

1. At the end of the w_____k, Ellie's class went on a field trip. (ee, ie)

2. They went to a p_____ch orchard out in the country. (ie, ea)

3. There were all kinds of f_____lds and farms near the orchard. (ee, ie)

4. Looking out the windows of the bus, the students saw dozens of wh_____t fields. (ea, ee)

5. They watched the stalks blow in the br_____ze. (ea, ee)

6. At the Gregors' farm, the peach tr_____s were full of fruit. (ie, ee)

7. Ellie and her friend, Omar, each picked thirt_____n peaches. (ee, ea)

8. The owner, Mrs. Gregor, said that a th_____f visits the orchard every night. (ea, ie)

9. Ellie and Omar laughed when they found out that it is a raccoon who st_____ls the fruit. (ie, ea)

10. When Mr. Zhou's class got back to school, they learned how to make a r_____l peach pie. (ea, ee)

11. They had to kn_____d the dough for only a few minutes. (ie, ea)

12. Mr. Zhou's class ate the warm pie with vanilla b_____n ice cr_____m. (ee, ea)

13. Everyone agr_____d it was the best field trip of the year. (ee, ie)

Lesson 1.20 Vowel Sounds (ind, ild, igh)

The vowel **i** can make a long sound when it is followed by the letters **nd**, **ld**, or **gh**.

find beh**ind**   **wild** ch**ild**   s**igh** n**igh**t

Read each meaning below. Choose a word from the box that matches the meaning. Write the word on the line.

blind   flashlight   wild   tight   thigh   behind   midnight   kind   child   mind

1. _____ the opposite of loose

2. _____ the part of the leg that is above the knee

3. _____ not tame; out of control

4. _____ 12 o'clock in the evening

5. _____ not able to see

6. _____ nice; sweet

7. _____ a young person

8. _____ the opposite of in front of

9. _____ something held in the hand that can help you see at night

10. _____ another word for brain

Lesson 1.20 Vowel Sounds (ind, ild, igh)

Read each sentence below. Complete the sentence with a word that rhymes with the word in parentheses ( ). The word you choose should make sense in the sentence.

1. My sister is the last _____ in a family of eight. (mild)

2. Austin said to make a _____ turn at the stop sign. (knight)

3. Uncle David has to _____ the old grandfather clock every few weeks. (mind)

4. The Simons had to _____ the house with candles when they lost power during the storm. (bright)

5. Did you follow the clues and _____ the treasure? (blind)

6. The books on the top shelf are too _____, and Parker cannot reach them. (sigh)

7. A new year begins at _____ on January 1st. (flashlight)

8. Three _____ bunnies live in Grandma's backyard and snack on the lettuce. (child)

Read the words below. One word in each set does not belong. Circle the word that has a different vowel sound than the others.

1. sigh   sing   right   5. rind   flip   fright

2. whip   grind   wild   6. chin   child   flight

3. mind   slight   sling   7. blind   bright   bit

4. tight   mild   trip   8. fight   hint   hind

Review Vowel Sounds

> - **Ai**, **ay**, and **ei** can all make the long **a** sound, as in sn**ai**l, m**ay**, and v**ei**n.
> - **Ee**, **ea**, and **ie** can all make the long **e** sound, as in j**ee**p, m**ea**t, and n**ie**ce.
> - **Oa** and **ow** can make the long **o** sound, as in c**oa**t and gr**ow**n.
> - The vowel **o** plus **ld** or **st** can make a long **o** sound, as in t**old** and p**ost**.
> - The vowel **i** plus **nd**, **ld**, or **gh** can make a long **i** sound, as in f**ind**, ch**ild**, and s**igh**.

Look at the pictures below. On the first line, write the word that names each picture. Then, write the word from the box that rhymes with each picture name.

| peach | glow | rail | tray | bold | float | weight | sigh | three |

Read the words below. One word in each set does not belong. Circle the word that has a different vowel sound than the others.

1. post   mold   sail
2. bay   freeze   cheat
3. wild   rip   flight
4. flap   fail   stray

Review Vowel Sounds

Read the paragraphs below. Each of the words in bold has a long vowel sound. Listen to the vowel sound and write each word in bold beside the correct heading.

The **sea** horse is a type of fish, but it probably looks different from any fish you've ever **seen**. Its head is shaped like a horse's head, which is how the sea horse got its name. Some people think the sea horse looks like a chess **piece** called a **knight**. Its body is covered with bony plates and small spines. The tip of its tail curls and can be used for clinging to plants.

Sea horses live in warm water. They are **weak** swimmers, so they don't usually go into **deep** water. Unlike most animals, the male is in charge of the eggs. He **keeps** them in his pouch until they are ready to hatch. Sea horses are also different from other fish because they swim **upright**.

Sea dragons are a member of the same family as sea horses. Sea dragons have long fins that flow around them. Some people think these fins look like **leaves**. The flowing fins help them hide in **fields** of seaweed that **sway** back and forth with the waves.

Project Sea Horse is one group that **feels** sea horses **need** to be protected. They are often caught in the **wild** by fishermen. Sometimes, they are used in making medicine. Sometimes, they are sold as pets. Project Sea Horse wants to **teach** the world about these interesting creatures. They hope the sea horses will **stay** around for a long time to come.

long **e** as in p**ea**: _____ _____ _____ _____

long **e** as in b**ee**p: _____ _____ _____ _____ _____

long **e** as in ch**ie**f: _____ _____

long **i** as in n**igh**t: _____ _____

long **i** as in ch**ild**: _____

long **a** as in d**ay**: _____ _____

Lesson 1.22 Vowel Sounds (oo, ew)

- The letters **oo** can make the sound you hear in b**oo**t and bl**oo**m. They also make the sound you hear in g**oo**d and b**oo**k.
- The letters **ew** can make the sound you hear in fl**ew** and n**ew**s.

Look at the pictures below. Write the word that names each picture on the first line. On the second line, write a rhyming word.

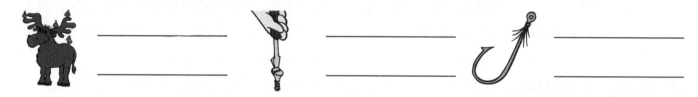

Read the paragraphs below. Circle the word from each pair that best completes the sentences.

You may not know who A. A. Milne is, but there is a (wood, good) chance you have read some of his (books, scoops). A (few, chew) of them have even been made into (spools, cartoons). Milne wrote the Winnie the (Pooh, Hood) books that children around the world know and love. He wrote the stories for his young son, Christopher. The characters in the books are based on Christopher's toys. Pooh was one of Christopher's stuffed bears. Kanga was a mother (moose, kangaroo), and Roo was her baby. Another character was a (moon, gloomy) donkey named Eeyore.

In most of the stories, Christopher Robin and his (goose, crew) of animal friends have adventures. Of course, the real Christopher Robin (few, grew) up over time. The Pooh stories end when the human boy goes to (school, mood) and becomes (new, too) old to play with his stuffed friends all day. No one (knew, noon) what a big hit A. A. Milne's nursery stories would be.

Lesson 1.22 Vowel Sounds (oo, ew)

Circle the two words in each set that have the same vowel sound.

1. chew   stew   chop   5. hoot   dew   hot

2. zoo   brown   drool   6. gloom   loop   crook

3. fleck   spoon   flew   7. foot   noon   hood

4. stood   brook   new   8. book   goose   snooze

Read the paragraphs below. Pay careful attention to the sentences in bold. Circle the words in those sentences that have the **oo** or **ew** spelling.

The harvest moon can be seen around September 23 every year. It appears during the fall equinox. An equinox is the time of year when day and night are the same length.

The harvest moon looks bigger than other full moons. This is because it hangs low in the sky. **The moon is always the same size, but it just seems to loom bigger during the harvest moon.** It also rises not long after sunset.

The harvest moon got its name from farmers. **It took them a long time to harvest crops in the fall. It was good for the farmers to have the extra light. They knew they would have more time to harvest their crops, because the big, yellow moon lit up the fields.**

Did you know that the full moons of other months have names too? Naming moons is not a new idea. It is one way people kept track of time before today's calendars. **Some other moon names are Corn Moon, Wolf Moon, Hunter's Moon, Snow Moon, and Flower Moon.** Can you guess how they got their names?

Lesson 1.23 Vowel Sounds (au, aw)

> • The letters **au** can make the sound you hear in s**au**ce and c**au**ght.
> • The letters **aw** can make the sound you hear in dr**aw** and l**aw**n.

Read each word in bold. Circle the word beside it that has the same vowel sound.

1. **claw**	bawl	cast	bowl		5. **yawn**	slaw	sail	wow
2. **taught**	tank	law	wind		6. **straw**	hay	launch	ant
3. **fault**	caught	fat	fume		7. **auto**	tame	gnaw	runt
4. **jaw**	jail	cow	dawn		8. **shawl**	shop	tan	raw

Read each clue below. On the line, write the word from the box that matches the clue.

| August | straw | yawn | author | paw | fawn | crawl | auto | saw | lawn |

1. _____ the way babies move around

2. _____ the green grassy area around a house

3. _____ another word for writer

4. _____ something you do when you feel sleepy

5. _____ the month that comes between July and September

6. _____ an animal's foot

7. _____ another name for car

8. _____ a sharp tool used for cutting wood

9. _____ a young deer

10. _____ a long, skinny tube that you put in a glass and drink from

Lesson 1.23 Vowel Sounds (**au, aw**)

Look at the pictures below. Fill in the blanks to complete each picture name.

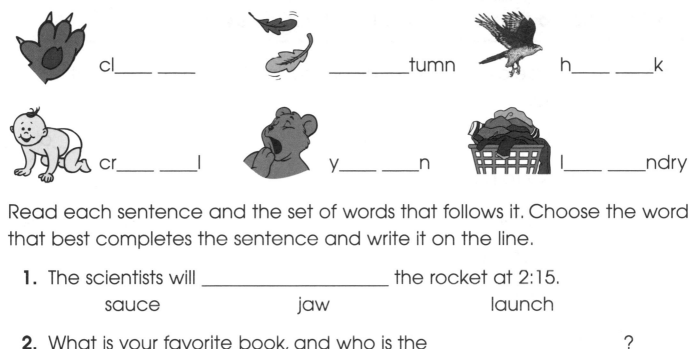

cl___ ___   ___ ___tumn   h___ ___k

cr___ ___l   y___ ___n   l___ ___ndry

Read each sentence and the set of words that follows it. Choose the word that best completes the sentence and write it on the line.

1. The scientists will _____ the rocket at 2:15.
   sauce   jaw   launch

2. What is your favorite book, and who is the _____?
   author   auto   shawl

3. Daniel's grandma _____ him how to count to ten in Spanish.
   awful   taught   fawn

4. We can't ride our bikes _____ it's raining.
   because   caution   fault

5. Habib put together a _____ puzzle with 150 pieces.
   awful   draw   Jigsaw

6. Callie's favorite dish at the diner is _____ and pancakes.
   slaw   sausage   drawn

Lesson 1.25 Vowel Sounds (**ou**, **ow**)

- The letters **ou** make the sound you hear in pr**ou**d and sh**ou**t.
- The letters **ow** make the sound you hear in n**ow** and t**ow**n.

Look at each picture below. On the line, write the word that names the picture. Then, circle the word that rhymes with the picture name.

_____   _____   _____

proud   now   cod   count   brown   old   hunt   how   blouse

Read the sentences below. Choose the word from the pair in parentheses ( ) that best completes each sentence. Write it on the line.

1. Charlie _____ is a popular character from the comic strip "Peanuts." (Brown, Flour)

2. The author of the comic, Charles Schultz, was _____ of the funny characters he created. (out loud, proud)

3. Charlie has terrible luck and seems to walk through life with a

   _____ hanging above his head. (count, cloud)

4. Charlie Brown has a clever _____ named Snoopy. (plow, hound)

5. Snoopy is known for sleeping on top of his _____. (doghouse, crown)

6. Charlie tries to kick the football. Lucy holds for him, but he usually ends

   up on the _____. (scout, ground)

Lesson 1.25 Vowel Sounds (**ou**, **ow**)

Read the clues below. Underline the word that matches each clue.

1. I am a word that describes someone who is grumpy or crabby.

    couch   grouch   sprout

2. I am a sound that wolves make. Dogs can make this sound, too. What am I?

    howl   mouse   ounce

3. I am a white or light brown powder used in baking. What am I?

    down   ground   flour

4. I am the face people make when they are sad. What am I?

    frown   sound   spout

5. I am a measurement of weight. What am I?

    out   pound   loud

6. I am the opposite of sweet. I am the flavor of lemons. What am I?

    town   sour   growl

7. I am what farmers must do to their fields before they plant. What am I?

    pout   bounce   plow

Read the words below. Circle the word that has the same vowel sound as the word in bold.

1. **now**   trout   newt   sold
2. **spout**   trust   scowl   mumps
3. **sound**   sun   rude   pouch
4. **brow**   gown   broil   gold
5. **crouch**   must   crunch   hour
6. **south**   booth   town   such
7. **cow**   rob   cute   growl

Lesson 1.26 The Sounds of y

- At the beginning of a word, the letter **y** can make the sound you hear in **y**ellow and **y**es.
- The letter **y** can make the long **i** sound, as in sp**y** and cr**y**.
- It can also make the long **e** sound, as in bell**y** and rust**y**.

Read each set of words below. Write **y**, long **i**, or long **e** on the line to show what sound the letter **y** makes in all the words in the set.

1. _____   tiny   quickly   story

2. _____   fly   dry   my

3. _____   sixty   chilly   candy

4. _____   yet   yak   yolk

5. _____   cry   sky   spy

6. _____   carry   windy   messy

7. _____   yourself yogurt   yank

Read the clues below. On the line, write the word that matches each clue. Make sure that the word you choose has the correct sound of **y**.

1. I am the number that comes after thirty-nine.
   (long **e**)   _____

2. I am the opposite of wet. (long **i**)   _____

3. People eat me on sandwiches with peanut
   butter. (long **e**)   _____

4. I am the opposite of old. (**y**)   _____

5. I am a coin worth one cent. (long **e**)   _____

6. I am the color of lemons and the sun. (**y**) _____

Lesson 1.26 The Sounds of y

Read the paragraphs below. Each of the words in bold contains the letter **y**. Listen to the sound the **y** makes. Write each word in bold under the correct heading. An example has been added below each heading to help you.

    Tyler got his first **yo-yo** when he was **only** four **years** old. It was a favor at a birthday **party**. Tyler liked the way the **shiny** red disks sparkled in the sun. When he picked it up, his hands knew just what to do.

    Five years later, Tyler is one of the best yo-yo players in the **city**. Just ask him to **try** a new trick, and watch the yo-yo **fly** into the air. Tyler can make all kinds of **tricky** moves look **easy**. He has videos of some of the most famous young yo-yo players in the **country**. When they **yank** the string with a flick of the wrist, the yo-yo goes **exactly** where they want it.

    Tyler hasn't gone to any competitions **yet**, but **lately** he has spent a lot of time practicing. He can do tricks like "hop the fence," "walk the dog," "rock the **baby**," and "over the falls." He might be **young**, but Tyler has all the makings of a true yo-yo champ.

long i	long e		y
by	thirsty	_____	yard
_____	_____	_____	_____
_____	_____	_____	_____
_____	_____	_____	_____
	_____	_____	_____
	_____	_____	_____

Lesson 1.27 R-Controlled Vowels (er, ir, ur)

When the letter **r** comes after a vowel, it can change the sound of the vowel. The letters **er**, **ir**, and **ur** can all make the same sound, as in p**er**ch, f**ir**m, and s**ur**f.

Look at the pictures below. Write the name of each picture on the line. Then, circle the pair of letters that make the /ur/ sound.

 _____

 _____

◯ _____

 _____

_____ _____

Read each word. Write the letter of its definition on the line.

1. _____ mother
2. _____ circus
3. _____ birthday
4. _____ purple
5. _____ verb
6. _____ purr
7. _____ winter
8. _____ germ
9. _____ fur
10. _____ stir

a. the day of the year a person was born
b. a part of speech that shows action
c. a cold, snowy season
d. something very tiny that can make you sick
e. a woman who has children
f. the color that is a mix of red and blue
g. the hair that covers an animal's body
h. to mix or blend
i. a show with clowns, animals, and the trapeze
j. a noise cats make when they are happy

Lesson 1.27 R-Controlled Vowels (er, ir, ur)

Read the sentences below. Write **ir**, **er**, or **ur** to complete the words. The words you form should make sense in the sentences.

1. The park near my house is quiet in wint_____.

2. The trees are bare, so I can see dozens of b_____ds p_____ched in the branches.

3. The wat_____ in the riv_____ doesn't freeze because it moves so quickly.

4. I love watching deer b_____st through the woods with their white tails bouncing along behind them.

5. Last Th_____sday, I saw a moth_____ deer and her baby come to the river to drink.

6. I've even seen a couple of t_____keys walking along the edge of a field.

7. When snowflakes start to tw_____l and wh_____l through the air, I know it's time to head for home.

8. Oth_____ people might prefer warm weath_____, but there's nothing like winter at the park for me.

Underline the letters that make the /ur/ sound in each word in bold below. Then, circle the word beside it that has the same sound.

1. **herd**	shirt	head	red
2. **perk**	peck	under	itch
3. **purse**	must	girl	punch
4. **birthday**	pig	wrist	fern
5. **curve**	chirp	cut	rug
6. **dirty**	mist	nest	person

Lesson 1.28 R-Controlled Vowels (ar, or)

When the letter **r** comes after a vowel, it can change the sound of the vowel.
- The letters **ar** can make the sound you hear in p**ar**ty and ch**ar**m.
- The letters **or** can make the sound you hear in f**or**k and sp**or**t.

On the first line, write the word that names each picture below. Then, write the words from the box under the heading with the same vowel sound.

| thorn | arch | cart | sport | scar | tart | porch | cord |

_____   _____

_____   _____   _____   _____

_____   _____   _____   _____

Read the definitions below. On the line, write the word from the box that matches each definition.

| snore | garden | fork | yarn | large | north |

1. the opposite of small   _____

2. an area where people grow flowers and plants   _____

3. a piece of silverware used for spearing food   _____

4. a type of thick thread or string used for knitting   _____

5. a noise that some people make when they sleep   _____

6. the opposite of south   _____

Lesson 1.28 R-Controlled Vowels (ar, or)

Read the paragraphs below. Underline the word from each pair in parentheses ( ) that best completes the sentences.

Have you ever gone to a (farmers', marchers') market? They can be a great place to visit on a Saturday (porch, morning). Some are located near (cars, farms) in the country. Others are right in the middle of cities. One reason people enjoy shopping at (markets, scarves) instead of (sports, stores) is that everything they buy is so fresh. Sometimes, it is also less expensive. If you buy a tomato that had (far, for) to travel before it reached your grocery store, you will be (charged, formed) more (fort, for) it.

At a farmers' market, you can buy things that are in season and grown nearby. How about some (large, sharp), ripe peaches, crisp cucumbers, or sweet (cork, corn)? Many markets sell (more, sort) than just fruits and vegetables. For example, you may be able to buy organic meat, like (horn, pork) or chicken. Organic means that the animals ate only natural foods. (Organic, Morning) vegetables are not sprayed with chemicals. Other markets have (arts, marks) and crafts or baked goods for sale.

Do you have a (garden, harp) at home? If you live in a city, there may be a community garden nearby. If you grow more vegetables or flowers than you can use, think about taking your extras to a farmers' market. All you need is a (march, cart) or a stand. Your business may (yarn, start) out small and grow (larger, shorter) every week!

Review The Sounds of **y** and **r**-Controlled Vowels

Read the clues below. Circle the word that matches each clue.

1. I am a piece of clothing worn around the neck in cold weather. What am I?

   skirt   scarf   sport

2. I am a person who doesn't like to be seen. Sometimes, I go undercover and secretly watch people. What am I?

   happy   spy   shy

3. I am the opposite of the word before. What am I?

   under   verb   after

4. I am an animal that people ride. I make the sound neigh. You can find me on a farm. What am I?

   horse   bird   river

5. I am the group of people you are related to. What am I?

   family   happy   quickly

6. I am like a sweet potato. I can be baked or mashed. What am I?

   yacht   yellow   yam

7. I am usually made of glass. I can be used for storing things, like jam or sauce. What am I?

   jar   stork   porch

8. I am something you might write to a friend. I usually begin with the word dear.

   term   other   letter

9. I am the yellow part of an egg. What am I?

   sunny   yolk   yogurt

10. I am a reptile. I carry my shell on my back for protection. What am I?

    germ   fern   turtle

Review The Sounds of **y** and **r**-Controlled Vowels

Draw a line from each word in bold to the word beside it that has the same **r**-controlled vowel sound.

		verse			torch
1.	**third**	shore	**5.**	**chore**	shop
		think			jar

		dash			mutt
2.	**marsh**	star	**6.**	**curl**	chart
		clerk			germ

		cut			fort
3.	**curb**	short	**7.**	**spark**	bag
		shirt			dart

		mark			cost
4.	**torn**	cork	**8.**	**core**	sword
		tug			trust

Read the sentences below. Circle words that contain the letter **y**. On the line, write the sound of **y** you hear (**y**, long **i**, or long **e**) in the words you circled.

1. After I dry this pan, I'm going to fry the fish I caught with my dad. _____

2. The baby bunny was lucky to find crisp lettuce in the pretty garden. _____

3. Yesterday, Yoko yelled when she got stung by a yellow jacket. _____

4. Aaron will fly his kite high in the sky at the park. _____

Lesson 2.1 Base Words and Endings (-**ed**, -**ing**)

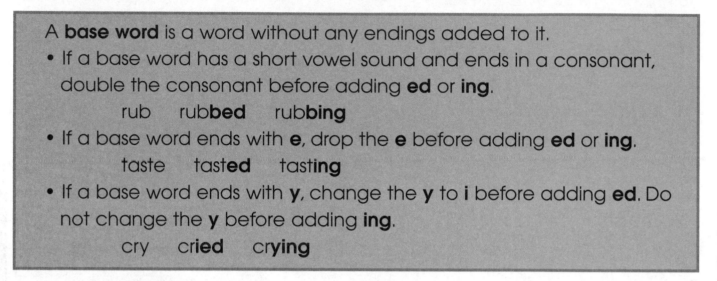

A **base word** is a word without any endings added to it.
- If a base word has a short vowel sound and ends in a consonant, double the consonant before adding **ed** or **ing**.
    rub   rub**bed**   rub**bing**
- If a base word ends with **e**, drop the **e** before adding **ed** or **ing**.
    taste   tast**ed**   tast**ing**
- If a base word ends with **y**, change the **y** to **i** before adding **ed**. Do not change the **y** before adding **ing**.
    cry   cr**ied**   cry**ing**

Fill in the blanks in the chart below.

Base Word	Add ed	Add ing
	chopped	
		hiking
bloom		
plan		
		spying
hope		
		humming
carry		
	suggested	
		clapping
try		
		acting
hug		

Lesson 2.1 Base Words and Endings (-**ed**, -**ing**)

Read the paragraphs below. Underline the word from the pair in parentheses ( ) that correctly completes each sentence.

Ellis Island is (located, locateed) in New York Harbor. Immigrants, or people (moveing, moving) to the United States from other countries, usually passed through Ellis Island. They had to be (interviewed, interviewd) before they were (allowing, allowed) to enter the country. They also had to be (examined, examineed) by a doctor to make sure they were healthy. If relatives of yours came to America from Europe during the early 1900s, they probably (passed, passing) through Ellis Island.

People who were (traveled, traveling) by boat could see the Statue of Liberty as they made their way into New York Harbor. Some people (cried, cryed) when they first saw it. Ellis Island and the famous statue were both signs to immigrants that their new life was (started, starting). Today, there is a museum on Ellis Island. If you are interested in (seing, seeing) whether any relatives of yours (stopped, stoped) at Ellis Island, you can try checking the passenger list at www.ellisisland.org.

Read the sentences below. Write the base word for each word in bold.

1. Elizabeth made a family tree when her class **studied** Ellis Island.

   _____

2. After **quizzing** her mom, she did some research on the Internet.

   _____

3. Elizabeth learned that her great-grandparents had **lived** in Ireland.

   _____

4. They were **married** when they were only 17 years old.

   _____

Lesson 2.3 Comparative Endings (-**er**, -**est**)

• The endings -**er** and -**est** can be added to base words to make a comparison.

> Add **er** to mean more.   loud**er** = more loud
> Add **est** to mean most.   loud**est** = most loud

• For words that end in **e**, drop the **e** and add **er** or **est**.

> wise   wis**er**   wis**est**

• For words that end in a consonant and **y**, change the **y** to **i** before adding **er** or **est**.

> funny   funn**ier**   funn**iest**

• For words that have a short vowel sound and end in a consonant, double the consonant before adding **er** or **est**.

> big   big**ger**   big**gest**

Read the sentences below. On the line, write the comparative form of the words in parentheses ( ).

1. The _____ place in the world that people live is Dallol, Ethiopia. It can be 145 degrees in the sun! (most hot)

2. Aswan, Egypt, is the _____ place in the world, with only $\frac{2}{100}$ of an inch of rain each year. (most dry)

3. Mt. Waialeale, Hawaii, is the _____ place in the United States. It gets about 460 inches of rain per year. (most wet)

4. Mt. Waialeale is _____ than Mt. Washington, New Hampshire. (more wet)

5. It is _____ in Yuma, Arizona, than in Las Vegas, Nevada. (more sunny)

6. Resolute, Canada, is one of the _____ places people live. Only about 200 people stay there all year long. (most cold)

Lesson 2.3 Comparative Endings (-**er**, -**est**)

Fill in the blanks with the correct form of the comparative word.

Base Word	Add er	Add est
	safer	
thin		
sweet		sweetest
		warmest
strange		
busy		

Read the sentences below. Underline the word in each pair that correctly completes the sentence.

1. The Boxley family has six cats. Brady is the (friendliest, friendlier).
2. Besty is (quietest, quieter) than Blossom and Bridget.
3. Benjamin is the (largeest, largest) cat.
4. Blaze is (gentler, gentlest) than his brothers and sisters.
5. Blossom has bright orange fur and is definitely the (fluffyest, fluffiest) cat.
6. Bridget is a picky eater, so she is (thinner, thiner) than the others.
7. Mrs. Boxley thinks Blaze is (smarter, smartest) than Brady and Benjamin.

Phonics Connection

Write beginning **l** blend and **r** blend words from the sentences above.

l blend: _____ _____ _____

r blend: _____ _____ _____

_____ _____ _____

Lesson 2.4 Plurals

The word **plural** means more than one.
- To make most words plural, just add **s**.   book book**s**   bell bell**s**
- If a noun ends in **sh, ch, s**, or **x**, add **es**.   fox fox**es**   bush bush**es**
- If a noun ends with a consonant and **y**, drop the **y** and add **ies**.
  fly fl**ies**   city cit**ies**
- For some words that end in **f** or **fe**, change the **f** or **fe** to **v** and
  add **es**.   wolf wol**ves**   loaf loa**ves**

Look at the pictures below. On the first line, write the word that names each picture. On the second line, write the plural form of the word.

Read the sentences below. On the line, write the correct plural form of the word in parentheses ( ).

1. The park was filled with the _____ of Little League players. (family)

2. Each of the _____ gave their teams a few last words of advice. (coach)

3. Alex, the Cougars' pitcher, wound up and nodded at his

   _____ (teammate)

4. Clare hit the ball and ran two _____ before she was tagged out. (base)

Lesson 2.4 Plurals

Write the word from the box that matches each clue below. Then, find the plural form of each word in the puzzle. Circle the words you find.

| spoon | class | leaf | diary | party | thief | peach | pony | dolphin |

1. _____ an event where people get together to celebrate

2. _____ someone who steals things

3. _____ a piece of silverware used for eating soup

4. _____ a small horse

5. _____ a sweet, pale-orange summer fruit

6. _____ a friendly gray mammal that lives in the ocean

7. _____

a group of children who go to the same school and have the same teacher

8. _____

a book in which people record the things that happen to them

9. _____

the small, flat green part of a plant or tree

t	h	i	e	v	e	s	j	x	s
h	e	p	e	a	c	h	e	s	a
n	d	o	l	p	h	i	n	s	u
r	i	n	e	t	h	x	c	q	a
c	a	l	g	a	t	o	l	r	k
b	r	e	u	d	n	y	a	a	s
o	i	s	p	o	o	n	s	t	t
f	e	k	t	f	p	j	s	o	b
y	s	r	l	e	a	v	e	s	v
w	p	a	r	t	i	e	s	d	l

Lesson 2.6 Possessives

> A **possessive** is a word that shows ownership. Adding an apostrophe
> (') plus **s** to a word makes it possessive.
>   Dante**'s** jacket   Mr. Fargo**'s** mail   the shirt**'s** collar
>
> Even when a singular word ends in **s**, add **'s** to form the possessive.
>   the boss**'s** desk   Tess**'s** backpack   Dr. Jones**'s** office

Read each phrase below. On the line, write the possessive form.

1. the homework of Will _____

2. the tail of the squirrel _____

3. the keyboard of the computer _____

4. the gym of the school _____

5. the eyes of Charles   _____

6. the actors of the movie _____

7. the books of the library _____

8. the smile of Malika _____

9. the colors of the dress _____

Read the sentences below. If the word in bold is plural, write **PL** on the line.
If it is possessive, write **PO**.

1. _____ The trapeze **artists** flew through the air.

2. _____ The **lion's** roar shook the seats in the circus tent.

3. _____ The elephants ate **peanuts** from their trainer's hand.

4. _____ The **clown's** nose was round and red.

5. _____ The **ringmaster's** routine made the fans laugh.

Lesson 2.6 Possessives

> Add an apostrophe (') to the end of a plural word to form a **plural possessive**.
>
> the girls' books   the monkeys' food   the teachers' classrooms
>
> If a plural word does not end in **s**, add an apostrophe plus **s** ('**s**).
> the children**'s** lunch   the people**'s** votes   the men**'s** ideas

Read each phrase below. On the line, write the plural possessive.

1. the tents of the campers _____

2. the sleeping bags of the boys _____

3. the flames of the campfires _____

4. the chirping of the crickets _____

5. the singing of the children _____

6. the zippers of the backpacks _____

7. the beams of the flashlights _____

8. the smells of the food _____

Phonics Connection

In the exercise above, five words contain digraphs. Write the words on the lines below and circle the digraphs.

_____   _____   _____

_____   _____

Lesson 2.6 Possessives

Read each phrase below. If it is plural, write **PL** on the line. If it is singular possessive, write **SP**. If it is plural possessive, write **PP**.

1. _____ Jack's canary

2. _____ the cats' water bowl

3. _____ the baby gerbils

4. _____ Akiko's guinea pig

5. _____ the Stosaks' turtles

6. _____ the lizards' cage

7. _____ the barking sheepdogs

8. _____ the rabbit's foot

Read the sentences below. Circle the letter of the word that correctly completes each sentence.

1. Eliza is watching the _____ pets while they are out of town.

   a. Howells'

   b. Howells's

2. _____ job is to feed the goldfish and the hamsters, Harriet and Hank.

   a. Elizas

   b. Eliza's

3. The _____ cage is filled with cedar chips.

   a. hamster's

   b. hamsters

4. Eliza drops flakes of food into the _____ tank.

   a. goldfish's

   b. goldfishes's

Phonics Connection

In the first exercise above, three words begin with hard **c**. One word begins with hard **g** and one begins with soft **g**. List the words below.

Hard c: _____ _____ _____

Hard g: _____

Soft g: _____

Lesson 2.6 Possessives

Rewrite each sentence, replacing the words in bold with a possessive.

1. The **teacher of the sisters** is Mrs. Huong.

   _____

2. The **schedule for the bus** is posted on the bulletin board.

   _____

3. The lyrics are on the inside of **the case of the CD**.

   _____

4. **A friend of Antoine** will be here at noon.

   _____

5. The **pieces of the game** are still inside the box.

   _____

6. The **wings of the butterflies** seem to shimmer in the sunlight.

   _____

7. Be careful not to let go of **the strings of the balloons**.

   _____

8. The **frame of the painting** is cracked.

   _____

9. The **jackets of the skaters** were warm and cozy.

   _____

10. The **ring of the alarm clock** is loud and shrill.

   _____

Review Plurals and Possessives

Fill in the blanks to complete the chart below. The first row is done for you.

Singular	Plural	Singular Possessive	Plural Possessive
book	books	book's	books'
woman			women's
	wolves	wolf's	
egg			eggs'
library		library's	
sheep		sheep's	
	mice		mice's
dish			dishes'
		city's	cities'

On the first line, write the plural form of each word. On the second line, write a phrase using the plural possessive form.

Example: bike   bikes _____   bikes' tires _____

1. school   _____   _____

2. bus   _____   _____

3. leaf   _____   _____

4. beach   _____   _____

5. country   _____   _____

6. computer   _____   _____

7. story   _____   _____

8. fox   _____   _____

Review Plurals and Possessives

Read the paragraph below. If the word in bold is plural, write **PL** on the line. If it is singular possessive, write **SP**. If it is plural possessive, write **PP**.

The highest waterfalls _____ in North America are in California's _____ Yosemite National Park. The falls _____ are 2,425 feet tall. That is about 13 times as tall as Niagara Falls. Yosemite is near the Sierra Nevada Mountains. In the spring, the mountains' _____ snow begins to melt. The melted snow fills the rivers _____ and feeds the waterfalls. By the end of summer, most of the park's _____ falls are pretty dry.

Read the sentences below. Underline the word that correctly completes each sentence.

1. John (Muir's, Muirs') dream was to preserve Yosemite as a national park.
2. Grizzly bears used to live in Yosemite, but no (grizzlys, grizzlies) are found there today.
3. Native American (tribes', tribes) lived in the area before explorers arrived.
4. The sequoia (trees', trees) trunks reach hundreds of feet into the air.
5. There are more than 250 (species, specieses) of animals at Yosemite.
6. (Grasses, Grass') in the meadows provide food for many animals.
7. (Hikeres, Hikers) can enjoy more than 800 miles of trails.
8. Thousands of (familys, families) visit the park every year.
9. It is not unusual to see (deers, deer), skunks, beavers, and raccoons.
10. Some lucky visitors even spot black bears or (wolves, wolfs).
11. The (rangers', rangeres) job is to watch over the park, the animals, and the visitors.

Lesson 2.8 Contractions

A **contraction** is a short way of writing two words. When the words are combined, an apostrophe (') takes the place of the missing letters.

I am = I'm   he will = he'll   we have = we've   is not = isn't

The words will and not form the contraction won't.

Draw a line to match the words on the left with their contractions.

1. he would		I'll
2. I will		she's
3. did not		you've
4. have not		haven't
5. she is		he'd
6. they are		weren't
7. were not		didn't
8. you have		they're

Read each sentence below. On the line, write the contraction for the words in bold.

1. Julia **has not** left the house in a week. _____

2. **She is** getting over the chicken pox. _____

3. Julia's case of the chicken pox **was not** as bad as Max's was. _____

4. **He will** be back in school next week, too. _____

5. Julia's mom told her she **should not** scratch too hard. _____

6. "**That is** easier said than done!" replied Julia. _____

Lesson 2.8 Contractions

Fill in the blanks to complete the problems below. Some problems have more than one correct answer. For example, **'d** can stand for had or would.

1. we + _____ = we're   6. it + _____ = it's

2. _____ + not = won't   7. _____ + not = couldn't

3. I + am = _____   8. I + have = _____

4. they + _____ = they'd   9. you + _____ = you're

5. she + has = _____   10. _____ + is = he's

Read the riddles below. Circle the contraction in each riddle. Then, write the two words that form the contraction.

1. **Q:** What did one eye say to the other?

   A: Don't look down, but something smells.

   _____ _____

2. **Q:** What runs around a house but doesn't move?

   A: A fence. _____ _____

3. **Q:** Why do hens lay eggs?

   A: Because If they dropped them, they'd break.

   _____ _____

4. **Q:** What kind of bird can't swim, fly, or catch a fish?

   A: A peli-can't. _____ _____

5. **Q:** What's the capital in France?

   A: F. _____ _____

Review Compound Words and Contractions

Look at the pictures below. Choose the compound word from the box that names each picture, and write it on the line.

| rainbow | bedroom | teacup | anteater | waterfall |
| cupcake | airplane | motorcycle | backpack | |

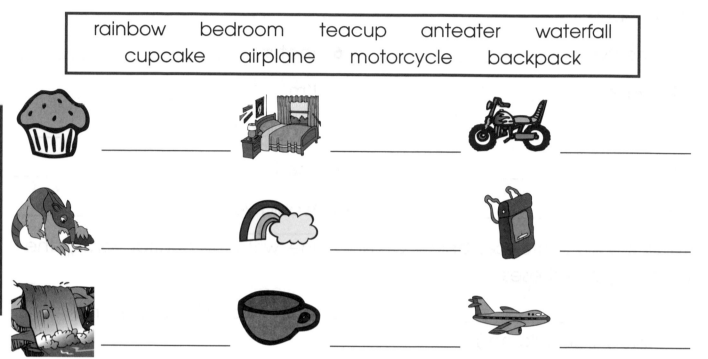

_____   _____   _____

_____   _____   _____

_____   _____   _____

Combine each word in bold with as many of the words in the box as you can to create compound words. Write the words on the lines. Hint: The words in bold will be the first part of each compound.

| works | flake | brush | bath | seat | shine | yard | burn |
| paste | fly | cage | bone | place | rise | storm | seed |

1. **back** _____   _____   _____

2. **bird** _____   _____   _____

3. **fire** _____   _____   _____

4. **sun** _____   _____   _____

5. **snow** _____   _____

6. **tooth** _____   _____

Review Compound Words and Contractions

Read the instructions below. Circle the six contractions. Underline the six different compound words.

Make a Homemade Windmill

Here's what you will need:

- a pencil with an eraser
- a ruler
- a square sheet of paper

- scissors
- a thumbtack

1. Draw a circle about two inches wide in the center of the piece of paper. Make a dot in the center of the circle.

2. Cut a straight line from each corner of the paper to the circle. Don't cut into the circle.

3. Bend every other point to the dot you drew in the center of the circle. It's important that the paper doesn't get folded when you bend it.

4. Hold the points together. Have a grownup stick the thumbtack through the points of paper and the center of the circle.

5. Push the tip of the thumbtack into the pencil eraser. The tack shouldn't be pushed all the way into the eraser.

6. When you blow gently on your windmill, it'll turn. Can you think of something other than wind that might be able to power a mill outside?

Lesson 2.9 Prefixes

A **prefix** can be added to the beginning of some words. Adding a prefix changes the meaning of a word.
- The prefixes **un-** and **dis-** both mean not.

   uneven = not even   **dis**honest = not honest

Add the prefix in parentheses ( ) to each base word below. Write the new word on the first line. On the second line, write the definition of the word.

1. (un) able   _____   _____

2. (dis) agree   _____   _____

3. (dis) like   _____   _____

4. (un) sure   _____   _____

5. (un) equal   _____   _____

6. (dis) trust   _____   _____

Add a prefix to each word below. Write the new word on the line. Then, write a sentence using the word you formed.

1. un + pack = _____

_____

2. dis + appear = _____

_____

3. un + plug = _____

_____

4. dis + obey = _____

_____

Lesson 2.9 Prefixes

• The prefixes **in-** and **im-** can mean not.

  indirect = not direct   **im**perfect = not perfect

Draw a line to match each word in column 1 with its definition in column 2.

1. impolite   not patient

2. incorrect   not complete

3. invisible   not correct

4. impatient   not possible

5. inexpensive   not polite

6. impossible   not exact

7. incomplete   not expensive

8. inexact   not visible

Read the sentences below. On the line, write a word from the box that best completes the sentence.

| impolite indoors impossible incorrect indirect impure |

1. Our plant needs _____ light, so don't put it directly in the sun.

2. It is _____ not to thank someone who holds a door open.

3. The scientist cannot use water that is _____ in her experiments.

4. Only one of your answers on the test was _____.

5. Please do not roller-skate _____!

6. If you believe in yourself, nothing in the world is _____.

Lesson 2.9 Prefixes

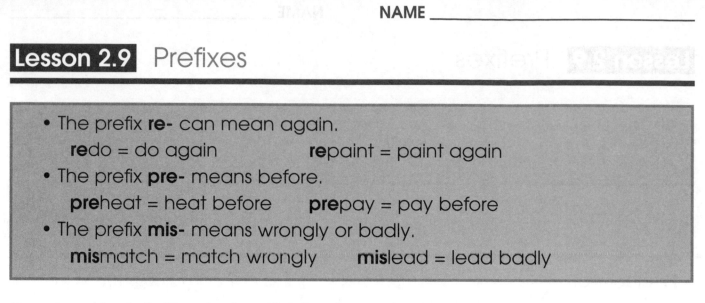

- The prefix **re-** can mean again.
    redo = do again   **re**paint = paint again
- The prefix **pre-** means before.
    preheat = heat before   **pre**pay = pay before
- The prefix **mis-** means wrongly or badly.
    mismatch = match wrongly   **mis**lead = lead badly

Read each definition below. Think of a matching word with the prefix **re-**, **pre-**, or **mis-** and write it on the line.

1. order before = _____

2. pack again = _____

3. read wrongly = _____

4. wash before = _____

5. check again = _____

6. mix before = _____

7. judge wrongly = _____

Add a prefix to each base word below. Write the new word on the first line. On the second line, write the definition of the word.

1. re + count = _____ _____

2. pre + dawn = _____ _____

3. mis + connect = _____ _____

4. pre + cook = _____ _____

5. re + sell = _____ _____

6. mis + name = _____ _____

Lesson 2.9 Prefixes

- The prefix **over-** means too much.
  overpay = pay too much   **over**flow = flow too much
- The prefix **under-** means too little or below.
  undercook = cook too little   **under**shirt = shirt worn below

Read the clues below. Each answer will contain the prefix **over-** or **under-**. Write your answer on the line.

1. The opposite of undercharge is _____.

2. The opposite of overweight is _____.

3. The opposite of overdress is _____.

4. The opposite of undercook is _____.

5. The opposite of overrate is _____.

6. The opposite of undersize is _____.

Read each sentence below. On the line, write a word from the box to take the place of the words in bold.

| overslept   underground   overthink   overrated   underwater   underline |

1. Can you open your eyes **below the water**? _____

2. The last book I read was **rated too high**. _____

3. Put a **line below** each compound word. _____

4. Do not **think too much** about your answer. _____

5. Brandon's alarm did not go off, so he
   slept too much. _____

6. The mole burrowed into its hole **below the ground**. _____

Lesson 2.10 Suffixes

Suffixes can be added to the ends of some words. A suffix changes the meaning of the word to which it is added.

• The suffix **-ly** means in a way. If a base word ends in **y**, change the **y** to **i** before adding **ly**.

slow**ly** = in a slow way   happy → happ**ily** = in a happy way

• The suffix **-y** means being or having. If a base word ends in **e**, drop the **e** before adding **y**.

Add the suffix in parentheses ( ) to each base word below. Use the new word in a sentence.

1. mess (y) _____

2. quick (ly) _____

3. bounce (y) _____

4. soft (ly) _____

5. easy (ly) _____

6. luck (y) _____

Read the definitions below. On the line, write the word that matches each definition.

1. in a strong way_____   **4.** having tricks _____

2. having rust _____   **5.** having steam _____

3. in a safe way _____   **6.** in a noisy way _____

Lesson 2.10 Suffixes

> • The suffixes **-er** and **-or** can mean a person who.
>
> writ**er** = a person who writes   act**or** = a person who acts

Read the sentences below. On the line, write a word with the suffix **-er** or **-or** to take the place of the words in bold.

1. When Carmen grows up, she hopes to be
    a person who teaches.   _____

2. Jill loves art class and knows that she will
    be **a person who paints**.   _____

3. Bailey lives near the ocean and plans to
    become **a person who sails**.   _____

4. Amina has hundreds of ideas for new things to
    make, so she wants to be **a person who invents**.   _____

5. Oliver's family has lived on a farm for 90 years,
    so he will be **a person who farms**.   _____

6. Andy dreams of being **a person who governs**.   _____

Write the meaning of each word on the line beside it.

1. sculptor = _____

2. collector = _____

3. gardener = _____

4. builder = _____

5. runner = _____

Lesson 2.10 Suffixes

- The suffix **-ful** means full of. If a base word ends in **y**, change the **y** to **i** before adding **ful**.

  room**ful** = a room full of   beauti**ful** = full of beauty

- The suffix **-less** means without.

  color**less** = without color   end**less** = without end

Read the clues below. Choose the word from the box that matches each clue. Write the answers in the numbered spaces in the crossword puzzle.

tasteful hopeless joyful careless peaceful spotless painless thankful

Across

2. without pain
4. full of thanks
7. without hope

Down

1. full of peace
3. without spots
4. full of taste
5. without care
6. full of joy

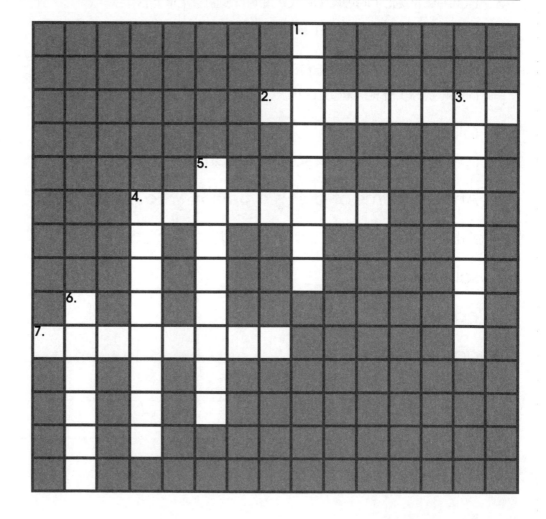

Lesson 2.10 Suffixes

> • The suffix **-able** means can be or able to be. If a base word ends in **e**, drop the **e** before adding **able**.
>
> enjoy**able** = able to be enjoyed   use → us**able** = able to be used
>
> • The suffix **-en** means made of or to make. If a base word ends in **e**, drop the **e** before adding **en**. For words that have a short vowel sound and end in a consonant, double the consonant before adding **en**.
>
> bright**en** = to make bright   loose → loos**en** = to make loose
>
> mad → madd**en** = to make mad

Read the sentences below. Add the suffix **-able** or **-en** to each word in parentheses ( ) so that it correctly completes the sentence.

1. The toy is made of soft plastic, so it is _____. (bend)

2. Be careful! Those plates are _____. (break)

3. Did Kayla find the _____ coins? (hid)

4. Doing pushups every day will _____ your muscles. (strength)

5. The _____ CD is on the desk. (broke)

Add a suffix to each base word below. Write the new word on the first line. On the second line, write the definition of the word.

1. hard + en = _____ _____

2. love + able = _____ _____

3. wash + able = _____ _____

4. wide + en = _____ _____

5. sharp + en = _____ _____

Review Prefixes and Suffixes

Adding a **prefix** to the beginning of a word can change the word's meaning.

- **un-, dis-, in-, im-** = not (**un**sure)
- **pre-** = before (**pre**school)
- **over-** = too much (**over**cook)
- **re-** = again (**re**start)
- **mis-** = wrongly or badly (**mis**read)
- **under-** = too little (**under**cook)

Beside each word, write the letter of its definition.

1. _____ invisible   **a.** charge too much

2. _____ overcharge   **b.** not even

3. _____ uneven   **c.** order before

4. _____ refill   **d.** not agree

5. _____ preorder   **e.** not visible

6. _____ disagree   **f.** fill again

Read the sentences below. Circle the word from the pair in parentheses ( ) that best completes each sentence.

1. The explorer Roald Amundsen was (undone, unafraid) of new challenges.

2. At first, he planned to explore the North Pole. He (removed, rethought) his plan when others got there first.

3. Amundsen (premixed, prearranged) a group of people who would travel with him.

4. The explorers packed everything they would need. They were careful not to (overload, overflow) themselves.

5. They were (unsure, unhealthy) if they would be first to reach the South Pole.

6. Amundsen was careful not to (mislead, misname) his group.

Review Prefixes and Suffixes

Adding a **suffix** to the end of a word can change the meaning of the word. Remember, sometimes the spelling of words that end in **y** or **e** must change before the suffix can be added.

- **-ly** = in a way (quick**ly**)
- **-er, -or** = a person who (writ**er**)
- **-less** = without (harm**less**)
- **-en** = made of or to make (soft**en**)
- **-y** = being or having (mess**y**)
- **-ful** = full of (cheer**ful**)
- **-able** = able to be (break**able**)

Add a suffix to each word below. Write the new word on the line. Then, write a sentence using the word you formed.

1. act + or = _____

_____

2. storm + y = _____

_____

3. beauty + ful = _____

_____

4. value + able = _____

_____

Read the definitions below. Write the word that matches each definition.

1. in a sleepy way   _____

2. without end   _____

3. to make dark   _____

4. able to be fixed   _____

5. a person who leads   _____

Lesson 2.11 Syllables

A **syllable** is part of a word and has one vowel sound. As you say a word, listen to the number of vowel sounds. This is the number of syllables the word has.

book = 1 vowel sound = 1 syllable

pic·ture = 2 vowel sounds = 2 syllables

for·ev·er = 3 vowel sounds = 3 syllables

Look at each picture below. Choose the word from the box that names the picture and write it on the first line. On the second line, write the number of vowel sounds you hear when you say the word out loud.

bicycle	monkey	tree
kangaroo	pretzel	balloon

Phonics Connection

1. Which two picture names have the vowel sound you hear in goose?

   _____   _____

2. Which two picture names begin with a two-letter blend?
   Circle the blend.

   _____   _____

NAME ____________________

Lesson 2.11 Syllables

Compound words can be divided into syllables between the two parts of the compound.

cup·cake book·case

A word that has two consonants between two vowels (like b**a**s**k**e**t**) can be divided between the consonants.

pen·cil nap·kin

A word that has a prefix can be divided between the prefix and the base word.

pre·wash mis·count

Read each word below. Say it to yourself and listen for the vowel sounds. Draw a slash (/) to divide each word into syllables.

1. airplane
2. dislike
3. picture
4. cookbook
5. refill
6. bathtub
7. beehive
8. preheat
9. lumber
10. undo

Read the sentences below. Use slashes to divide the words in bold into syllables.

1. On **Monday**, Cal went to the **dentist** because he had a **toothache**.
2. It was **winter**, so Cal could see his **footprints** in the snow on the **sidewalk**.
3. The **sunlight** was bright, and Cal was eager to get **indoors**.
4. "**Welcome** to Dr. Garcia's office," **someone** said.
5. Cal **untied** his boots and left them in the **hallway**.
6. He **disliked** cavities, but he loved going to Dr. Garcia's **office**.

Lesson 2.11   Syllables

Read the words in the box. Write each word below the correct heading.
Then, draw slashes (/) to divide the words into syllables.

| cucumber   wind   seashore   unlock   wonderful   bench |
| popular   shrimp   table   fish   star   terrible |
| ladder   breeze   adventure   silent   homesick   elephant |

1 syllable	**2 syllables**	**3 syllables**
_____	_____	_____
_____	_____	_____
_____	_____	_____
_____	_____	_____
_____	_____	_____

Read each word in bold. Circle the word beside it that has the same
number of syllables.

1. **grassy**	sniff	mitten	however
2. **difficult**	vacation	puzzle	jolly
3. **whale**	railroad	monster	sled
4. **pocket**	bush	before	bike
5. **multiply**	flavor	drive	factory
6. **cry**	pinch	different	fastest
7. **pumpkin**	paper	banana	climb
8. **water**	multiply	closed	hammer
9. **stomp**	trying	loose	crocodile

Lesson 2.11 Syllables

Read the sentences below. The words in parentheses ( ) will tell you which words to underline in the sentences.

1. When Hurricane Katrina hit the U.S. in 2005, it did a lot of damage. (3-syllable words)

2. Many people around the world wanted to help. (2-syllable words)

3. Three sisters in Maryland thought of a very special way to make a difference. (3-syllable words)

4. They started Project Backpack. (2-syllable words)

5. Jackie, Melissa, and Jenna Kantor collected backpacks full of things that kids along the Gulf Coast might need. (2-syllable words)

6. They quickly reached their goal of 1,000 backpacks. (1-syllable words)

7. Kids around the country heard about the project. (2-syllable words)

8. They collected backpacks in their own cities, too. (1-syllable words)

9. In two months, 50,000 backpacks were sent to kids who lived in the areas Katrina hit! (3-syllable words)

10. Even though the Kantor sisters were only 14, 11, and 8, they helped thousands of kids they had never even met. (2-syllable words)

Phonics Connection

1. Which word in number 2 has a **y** that makes the long **e** sound? _____

2. Which word in number 5 has the same vowel sound as blow? _____

3. Which word in number 6 has the hard **g** sound? _____

Review Syllables

Choose the word from the box that names each picture below and write it on the first line. On the second line, write the number of vowel sounds you hear when you say the word out loud.

REVIEW: CHAPTER 2 LESSON 11

| mosquito | banana | mailbox | pear | snowflake | wink |

Read the words below and fill in the blanks in the chart.

	Vowel Sounds Heard	Number of Syllables
rosebush		
crash		
misjudge		
redraw		
difficult		
washcloth		
crocodile		
plate		
pretzel		
corner		

Review Syllables

On the line, write the word that names the picture. Then, circle the word beside it that has the same number of syllables.

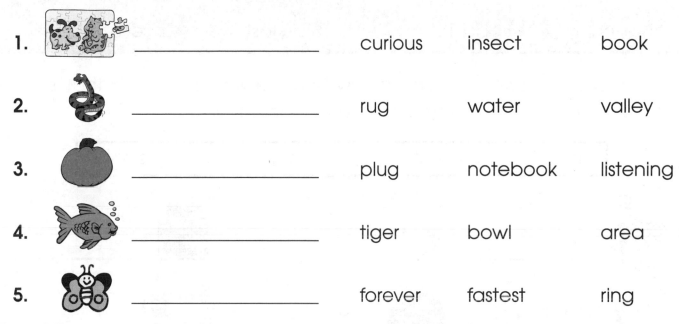

1. _____   curious   insect   book

2. _____   rug   water   valley

3. _____   plug   notebook   listening

4. _____   tiger   bowl   area

5. _____   forever   fastest   ring

Read the paragraphs below. Use slashes (/) to divide the words in bold into syllables.

    A **cactus** is a type of plant. It grows **mostly** in desert **areas** of the Americas. Cacti (the plural of cactus) are one of few plants that can live in the harsh **conditions** of deserts. **Unlike** most plants, cacti do not have leaves. **Instead**, they have sharp spines. The spines **protect** cacti from **desert animals**. Since plants usually lose **water** through their leaves, the spines help cacti save their water. Cacti also have thick, **fleshy** stems where they can store water. Their roots do not go deep **into** the ground like **other** plants. Instead, they spread out **over** a large space so they can get water from a **wider** area when it rains.

    There are **about** 1,700 **species** of cacti. One of the most interesting may be the saguaro cactus. It lives in the **Southwest** and in **Mexico** and can grow to be 50 feet tall!

Lesson 3.1 Synonyms

A **synonym** is a word that has the same or almost the same meaning as another word.

like, enjoy   dad, father   quick, fast   insect, bug

Look at each picture and label below. Find the word in the box that is a synonym for the picture name, and write it on the line.

| rabbit | present | rip | pail | hat | smile |

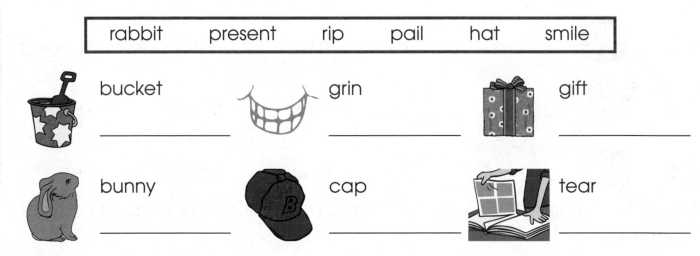

bucket
_____

grin
_____

gift
_____

bunny
_____

cap
_____

tear
_____

Read each clue and the choices below it. Circle the word that best matches the clue.

1. I am another word for great or wonderful.

    awful   terrific   old

2. I am another word for tired.

    sleepy   worried   joyful

3. I am another word for huge or enormous.

    tiny   slippery   giant

4. I am another word for wreck.

    move   push   destroy

5. I am another word for laugh.

    giggle   sigh   scream

Lesson 3.1 Synonyms

Draw a line to match each word in column 1 to its synonym in column 2.

1. end	beautiful
2. easy	mend
3. shut	near
4. pretty	finish
5. throw	simple
6. glad	close
7. jump	hop
8. close	toss
9. fix	happy

Read each sentence below. Find a synonym in the box for the word in bold and write it on the line.

see quiet pick broke small stop scream keep tug

1. Choose your three favorite flavors. _____

2. Tell Marissa to **pull** on the rope. _____

3. The house is **silent** in the middle of the night. _____

4. When did you **quit** taking ballet lessons? _____

5. The plate **shattered** when it hit the floor. _____

6. When Olivia walks we'll **shout** "Surprise!" _____

7. The sliver was so **tiny** I could barely see it. _____

8. Did you **watch** the game on TV last night? _____

9. Let's **save** the rest of the brownies for later. _____

Lesson 3.2 Antonyms

An **antonym** is a word that means the opposite of another word.

hard, soft   loud, quiet   new, old   right, wrong

Read the clues below. Fill in the blanks to complete the answer. Then, look for each answer in the word search puzzle. Circle the words you find.

1. the opposite of top   b___ ___ ___ ___ ___

2. the opposite of black   wh___ ___ ___

3. the opposite of enemy   fr___ ___ ___ ___

4. the opposite of evening   m___ ___ ___ ___ ___ ___

5. the opposite of up   d___ ___ ___

6. the opposite of love   h___ ___ ___

7. the opposite of over

    u___ ___ ___ ___

Phonics Connection

1. Which puzzle word contains a digraph?

    _____

2. Which puzzle word has a beginning blend?

    _____

n	m	r	u	n	d	e	r	v	a
q	d	b	b	j	a	r	h	p	l
b	o	t	t	o	m	c	a	z	x
o	w	p	l	y	o	e	t	g	i
j	n	u	n	f	r	i	e	n	d
s	d	r	t	n	n	q	o	a	p
d	g	m	w	h	i	t	e	w	n
r	z	t	t	w	n	o	u	n	h
e	g	c	f	e	g	r	h	n	e

Lesson 3.2 Antonyms

Read the paragraphs below. Choose an antonym from the box for each word in bold. Write it on the line beside the word.

slower	less	finished	bad	lost	easy
weaker	woman	short	smaller	fake	boring

American **tall** _____ tales were begun by pioneers of the Old West. Tall tales were a **good** _____ form of entertainment. TV did not exist, and books were **hard** _____ to get. Tall tales could be told to a group and passed from one person to the next. The main character of a tall tale is often someone who is **larger** _____ than life. The character is superhuman in some way and has wild adventures. In the story, he or she may be **stronger** _____, **faster** _____, smarter, or tougher than anyone else.

For example, have you ever heard the tale of John Henry? He could hammer railroad spikes faster than any **man** _____. He was **more** _____ than eight feet tall when he was born. He **started** _____ working on the railways when he was only three weeks old. When he raced against a machine, John Henry **won** _____. The tall tale is funnier and more interesting than the **real** _____ story could ever be.

Paul Bunyan, Annie Oakley, and Johnny Appleseed are other tall tale heroes you might know. What details make their stories so **exciting** _____?

Review Synonyms and Antonyms

Read each pair of words below. If the words are synonyms, write **S** on the line. If they are antonyms, write **A**.

1. _____ yell, whisper

2. _____ shout, scream

3. _____ easy, simple

4. _____ heavy, light

5. _____ like, enjoy

6. _____ wide, narrow

7. _____ funny, serious

8. _____ boat, ship

9. _____ tired, sleepy

10. _____ inside, outside

11. _____ city, town

12. _____ summer, winter

The word in parentheses ( ) will tell you to find a synonym or an antonym for each word below. Choose your answer from the box and write it on the line.

noisy full smooth lost west wrong infant find messy ill

1. neat (antonym) _____

2. empty (antonym) _____

3. missing (synonym) _____

4. sick (synonym) _____

5. right (antonym) _____

6. baby (synonym) _____

7. east (antonym) _____

8. loud (synonym) _____

9. locate (synonym) _____

10. rough (antonym) _____

Review Synonyms and Antonyms

Read the paragraphs below. Then, answer the questions that follow.

Have you ever visited a corn maze? The largest corn maze in the country is at the Richardson Farm in Spring Grove, Illinois. Every year, the family picks a new theme. An artist makes a drawing that goes with the theme. Then, the picture gets scanned into a computer. The lines of the picture are turned into the maze. When the corn on the farm is ten inches tall, the maze is cut into the fields. It's easier to cut the corn before it grows too tall.

In autumn, the Richardsons are ready for their first visitors to the maze. In 2004, the maze had pictures from Lewis and Clark's journey. In ten miles of trails, there were pictures of prairie dogs, bison (or buffaloes), and a traveler in a boat. Even though the trails are about ten miles long, you only have to walk about $\frac{1}{3}$ of a mile to solve a maze. What happens if you get lost? Don't worry, you'll be able to bring a map with you. You can also bring a cell phone to call the Richardsons for help if you get stuck.

1. Find an antonym for smallest in paragraph 1.   _____

2. Find a synonym for nation in paragraph 1.   _____

3. Find an antonym for old in paragraph 1.   _____

4. Find a synonym for creates in paragraph 1.   _____

5. Find an antonym for harder in paragraph 1.   _____

6. Find an antonym for shrinks in paragraph 1.   _____

7. Find a synonym for fall in paragraph 2.   _____

8. Find an antonym for last in paragraph 2.   _____

9. Find an antonym for short in paragraph 2.   _____

10. Find an antonym for found in paragraph 2.   _____

Lesson 3.3 Homophones

A **homophone** is a word that sounds the same as another word but has a different spelling and meaning.

It takes an *hour* to get there.   *Our* team won the game!

Tom will *be* late.   The *bee* landed on the pink flower.

Circle the word below each picture that correctly names it. Use a dictionary if you are not sure which homophone to choose.

bear   bare

shoo   shoe

I   eye

8

eight   ate

pear   pair

son   sun

knight   night

flour   flower

ant   aunt

Phonics Connection

There are three words in the exercise above that have a silent consonant pair. Write the words on the lines and circle the consonant pair in each word.

_____   _____   _____

Lesson 3.3 Homophones

Read each sentence below. The word in parentheses ( ) is a homophone for the word in bold. Write a sentence of your own using the homophone.

Example: Did Courtney **write** a story?

(right) Make a right turn at the light.

1. I **sent** Grandma an e-mail last week.

(cent) _____

2. What kind of **clothes** are you wearing to the party?

(close) _____

3. Alejandro will **meet** you at the park at noon.

(meat) _____

4. **Here** is the book I borrowed from you.

(hear) _____

Read the clues below. On the first line, write the word from box 1 that matches the clue. Then, find its homophone in box 2 and write it on the second line.

| road bye they're high four | | hi there buy for rode |

1. I am what people say when they are leaving.

_____   _____

2. I am the number that comes after three. _____ _____

3. I am the opposite of low. _____ _____

4. I am another name for street. _____ _____

5. I am a contraction for they are. _____ _____

Lesson 3.4 Multiple-Meaning Words

> A **multiple-meaning word** (also called a **homograph**) is a word that has more than one meaning.
> Can you help us?   George bought a can of tuna.
> Mia won the doll at the fair.   It's not fair that you have to go last.

Read each sentence below. On the line, write a sentence using another meaning of the word in bold. If you cannot think of another meaning, use a dictionary.

1. Did you drive or **fly** to Chicago?

   _____

2. The **bat** eats hundreds of mosquitoes every night.

   _____

3. The owl's wings are almost the same color as the **bark** of the tree.

   _____

4. On their first **date**, Abby's parents went to the movies.

   _____

5. Mrs. Kay needs one **yard** of fabric to make the costume.

   _____

6. We were late for school because we got stuck in a traffic **jam**.

   _____

7. How many pigs did you count in the **pen**?

   _____

8. Darren's dad works in a three-**story** building.

   _____

Lesson 3.4   Multiple-Meaning Words

Read each sentence and the definitions that follow. Circle the letter of the definition that matches the word in bold.

1. Nicholas and Matthew bought their dad a **watch** for his birthday.

    a. to look at

    b. a small clock worn on the wrist

2. There is a **pitcher** of lemonade on the counter.

    a. a container that holds liquid

    b. the person who pitches

3. Sanj's cold is gone and she feels **fine**.

    a. well; in good health

    b. money paid for breaking a law

4. The dentist gave Eric a pack of sugar-free **gum**.

    a. the flesh around your teeth

    b. a type of rubbery candy

5. The **kind** woman works at an animal shelter.

    a. nice; gentle; helpful

    b. a type or sort

6. A huge gust of **wind** knocked over the sign.

    a. to tighten by turning

    b. blowing air

7. How **close** is your school to your home?

    a. to shut

    b. near

8. Gabby came in **second** in the race.

    a. number two

    b. a measurement of time

Phonics Connection

Use the words in bold above to answer the following questions.

1. Which two words have the long **i** sound?

    _____   _____

2. Which two words have a silent consonant? Circle the consonant.

    _____   _____

Lesson 3.5 Figures of Speech

A **simile** is a comparison of two unlike things using the words like or as.
>   Lydia's cheeks were as red as cherries.
>   The sea sparkled like jewels in the morning sun.

A **metaphor** is a comparison of two unlike things without using like or as.
>   Alexander's heart was a steady drum beating in his chest.

Read each sentence below. If it contains a simile, write **S** on the line. If it contains a metaphor, write **M**.

1. _____ By dinnertime, Katsu will be as hungry as a bear.

2. _____ The tornado was a roaring train that sped across the field.

3. _____ Charlotte was a dolphin, diving and playing in the waves.

4. _____ Annie's new ideas were a breath of fresh air.

5. _____ The windows were like eyes that peered out from the front of

>   the house.

6. _____ Jake's dry hands were as rough as sandpaper.

7. _____ The fog was a blanket that covered the sleeping city.

8. _____ The water felt like ice to C. J. as he dove into the pool.

Use your imagination to complete each simile below.

1. Kelsey's eyes are as green as _____.

2. The lemon juice stung like _____ on Iman's paper cut.

3. The raspberries from the garden were as sweet as _____.

4. The pebbles were as smooth as _____ in Xavier's hand.

Lesson 3.5 Figures of Speech

Read the paragraphs below. Underline the four similes. Circle the two metaphors.

Fiona and Nora walked down the sandy path to the beach. It was the middle of the day, and the sand felt like hot coals under their bare feet. They walked faster, trying not to let their feet touch the sand for long. The water was a blue carpet stretching out toward the sky. It looked cool and inviting from the hot beach.

"It's beautiful here, isn't it?" said Nora. She turned her face to the sun that hung like a fat, yellow grapefruit in the sky. Nora sniffed the salty breeze. "The ocean air smells as fresh as clean laundry."

The girls found their parents and spread out their towels. They were careful not to wake their dad, who slept like a baby under a large umbrella. Suddenly, Fiona spotted a pelican. It was a missile zooming toward the water. A moment later, it flew away with a wriggling fish sticking out of its beak. "There's always something going on at the beach!" laughed Fiona.

Read the metaphors below. On the lines, tell which two things are being compared.

1. The 175-year-old house was a dinosaur.

   _____   _____

2. The stomachs of the teenage boys were bottomless pits.

   _____   _____

3. Marcus's legs were rubber as he walked onstage.

   _____   _____

Review Homophones, Multiple-Meaning Words, Figures of Speech

Circle the word below each picture that correctly names it. Use a dictionary if you are not sure which homophone to choose.

hair   hare

hoarse   horse

be   bee

dear   deer

ring   wring

mussel   muscle

Read each sentence below. Circle the homophone that correctly completes the sentence.

1. The department store is having a (sail, sale) on kids' clothes this week.

2. (Meat, Meet) me at the car in one (hour, our).

3. The mountain (peak, peek) is 1,700 feet above sea level.

4. (Your, You're) book report is really interesting.

Read the pairs of homophones below. Use each one in a sentence.

1. (wood, would) _____

_____

2. (one, won) _____

_____

3. (plain, plane) _____

_____

Review Homophones, Multiple-Meaning Words, Figures of Speech

Read the definitions and the sentences below. Make a check mark beside the sentence that uses the word in bold the same way as the definition.

1. **tear** = liquid that comes out of the eyes when crying

   ___ A **tear** rolled down the girl's cheek.   ___ Did you **tear** your shirt?

2. **seal** = a mammal that lives in the ocean and has flippers

   ___ **Seal** each letter before you mail it.   ___ The **seal** has thick, gray fur.

3. **rest** = to take a break or relax

   ___ Where are the **rest** of the children?   ___ **Rest** quietly until lunch.

4. **well** = a hole dug in the ground to get to water

   ___ We never use the old **well** in the yard.   ___ **Well**, I'm ready to go.

5. **box** = a square container

   ___ My uncle likes to **box** at the gym.   ___ What's inside the **box**?

Read each sentence below. Circle the two things that are being compared. Write **S** on the line if the comparison is a simile. Write **M** if it is a metaphor.

1. _____ The rain sounded like tiny footsteps racing across the roof.

2. _____ "Britta is the apple of my eye," said Grandpa proudly.

3. _____ The snow was a thick, white blanket on the rooftop.

4. _____ The heavy meal sat like a rock in Mr. Bloomberg's stomach.

5. _____ The children were quiet as mice as they waited.

Phonics Connection

Which three words in exercise 2 have the long **e** sound spelled **y**?

_____   _____   _____

Lesson 4.1 Alphabetical Order

Being able to place words in **alphabetical order**, or **ABC order**, can help you find what you are looking for in a dictionary, an encyclopedia, an index, or at the library.

When two words start with the same letter, use the second letter to decide the order. If the first two letters of the words are the same, use the third letter.

habit **j**eep **l**amb   **pa**sta **pe**st **pi**e   **da**rling **da**sh **da**te

Read each set of words. On the lines, number the words in ABC order.

1. _____ train

_____ uncle

_____ piano

2. _____ paste

_____ pass

_____ phase

3. _____ ear

_____ explain

_____ ever

4. _____ hem

_____ hey

_____ herd

5. _____ list

_____ kitten

_____ king

6. _____ mimic

_____ mint

_____ milk

Rewrite each list below so the words are in ABC order.

1. minnow, line, hers, mile _____

2. sloth, skunk, sleigh, sled _____

3. news, net, niece, nibble _____

Phonics Connection

1. Which word in exercise 1 begins with a digraph? _____

2. Which three words in exercise 2 begin with an **l** blend?

_____   _____   _____

Lesson 4.3 Entry Words

Read the paragraphs below. Write the entry word on the line beside each word in bold.

Julius Lester was born in Missouri in 1939. Julius's degree was in English, but he also **enjoyed** _____ music. He **recorded** _____ two albums, and he wrote a book about folk music. Later on, Julius wrote other **books** _____ for **adults** _____. They were not the books that would bring him great fame, though.

In the late 1960s, he **published** _____ two **children's** _____ books. One was called To Be a Slave and won an important award **called** _____ the Newbery Honor Medal. The other book was called Black **Folktales** _____. These two books were the start of an important **writing** _____ career for Julius Lester. So far, he has **written** _____ 25 books for **kids** _____! Most of his **stories** _____ deal with African-American history and folklore. Some of his books are The **Tales** _____ of Uncle Remus, John Henry, Sam and the **Tigers** _____, and How Many **Spots** _____ Does a Leopard Have and Other Tales.

Phonics Connection
Which two words in paragraph 1 have the same vowel sound as sport?

_____   _____

Review ABC Order, Guide Words, and Entry Words

REVIEW: CHAPTER 4 LESSONS 1–3

Rewrite the following list of authors' names in ABC order.

Cleary, Beverly _____

Lasky, Kathryn _____

Lowry, Lois _____

White, E. B. _____

Christopher, Matt _____

Babbitt, Natalie _____

Pinkney, Jerry _____

Banks, Lynne Reid _____

Byars, Betsy _____

Dahl, Roald _____

Wallace, Bill _____

On the line, write the word that names the picture. Circle the set of guide words that you would find on the same dictionary page as the picture name.

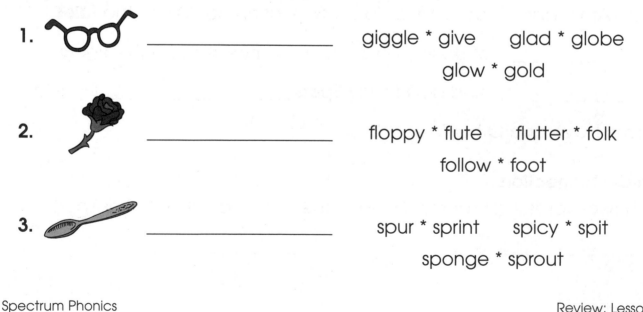

1. _____   giggle * give   glad * globe

   glow * gold

2. _____   floppy * flute   flutter * folk

   follow * foot

3. _____   spur * sprint   spicy * spit

   sponge * sprout

Review ABC Order, Guide Words, and Entry Words

Use the dictionary entries below to answer the questions.

story (stor' ee) pl. stories **1.** noun a made-up tale that entertains people
2. noun a floor or level of a building

spaniel (span' yul) noun a breed of dog that has droopy ears and silky fur

sparkle (spar' kul) verb to glitter or give off light

1. Put the entry words above in ABC order.

   _____   _____   _____

2. What is the plural form of story?   _____

3. What entry word would you use to find the
   definition of sparkling?   _____

4. Which of the words above would you find
   on a dictionary page with the guide words
   stopwatch and straw?   _____

5. Which word is a verb?   _____

6. Which definition of story is used in this sentence?
   Paco read his sister a story before bed.   _____

Rewrite the following words in ABC order.

1. recycle, rag, reflect, rain _____

2. cry, beach, slide, fling _____

3. feast, fan, father, fast_____

4. invite, ladybug, island, lamp_____

Answer Key

page 6

t; l; b
w; n; p

1. fan
2. book
3. fish
4. cake
5. sand
6. mail

page 7

1. dogs
2. walk
3. park
4. love
5. time
6. good

page 8

n; m; f
t, r, d

1. cat
2. skip
3. bug
4. wet
5. sag
6. shop
7. hid
8. cot

page 9

1. ss
2. ff
3. ll
4. ll; ss

5. ff; ff; ss
6. zz; ll; ss
7. ss

rat / rag / ran / rap
cut / cup / cub / cuff
pin / pill / pig / pit

page 10

1. HC
2. SC
3. SC
4. HC
5. SC
6. HC

1. SG
2. HG
3. SG
4. HG
5. HG
6. SG

page 11

Grocery List

grapes / celery / flour
cereal / clams / ice cream
carrots / oranges / sugar
gingerbread / milk / sliced bread
apples / lettuce / eggs
turkey / peanut butter / cat food

Look at each pair of pictures. Draw a line to match the hard or soft sound to each picture.

1. soft **g** — hard **g**
2. hard **c** — soft **c**
3. hard **c** — soft **g**
4. soft **c** — hard **g**

page 12

Hard C	Soft C
collects	circle
clay	place
plastic	price
countries	

circle
color
become
collector
club

Hard G	Soft G
glass	huge
grape	giants
games	age

page 13

1. frog
2. second
3. pencil
4. sugar
5. ice
6. cow
7. orange
8. cereal

page 14

t; b; k
ss; p; ll

1. near
2. beak
3. wings
4. hold
5. can
6. fast
7. look

page 15

1. garden — hard / soft
2. gym — hard / soft
3. attic — hard / soft
4. case — hard / soft
5. danger — hard / soft
6. slice — hard / soft
7. egg — hard / soft
8. edge — hard / soft

1. goat
2. cuddle
3. ceiling
4. geese
5. edge

Answer Key

6. coat
7. gust
8. cider
9. gel
10. crisp

page 16

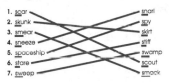
scarf; snowman; star; swing; spider; smile

1. sn
2. sk
3. sc
4. sp
5. st
6. sp
7. sw

page 17

1. scar — snarl
2. skunk — spy
3. smear — skirt
4. sneeze — stiff
5. spaceship — swamp
6. stare — scout
7. sweep — smack

stop; special; smoke; sniff; sky; smoke; swiftly; spark; skills

page 18

clock; blanket; plane; sled; flag; globe

1. planets
2. slow
3. flea
4. glue
5. cloud
6. blackboard
7. closet

page 19

lock	lip	low
block	blip	blow
clock	clip	flow
flock	flip	glow
	slip	plow
		slow

1. clubhouse; Answers will vary.
2. glad; Answers will vary.
3. blue; Answers will vary.
4. floor; Answers will vary.
5. flag; Answers will vary.
6. climbed; Answers will vary.
7. sleep; Answers will vary.
8. pledge; Answers will vary.

page 20

drew; from; try; dreamed; growing; gravel; from; creeks; bright; profit; traveled; promise

1. cr
2. tr
3. cr
4. gr
5. dr
6. gr

page 21

1. graze — brain
2. frost — truth
3. brave — droop
4. crow — grade
5. tractor — craft
6. drain — practice
7. pretzel — Friday

1. grandfather
2. price
3. green
4. friend
5. broom

6. crib
7. breakfast
8. principal
9. trash
10. crawl

page 22

snake; bread; spoon
claw; drum; fly

s blend	**l** blend	**r** blend
snail	plum	fruit
smoky	slime	pretty
scooter	slipper	trunk
slime	blaze	cry
slipper	floppy	drop
skunk	glass	bring

page 23

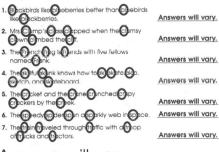
1. Blackbirds like blueberries better than bluebirds like blackberries. Answers will vary.
2. Mrs. Clump's class clapped when the clumsy clown climbed the cliff. Answers will vary.
3. The French frog is friends with five fellows named Frank. Answers will vary.
4. The skillful skunk knows how to skate, skip, sketch, and skateboard. Answers will vary.
5. The cricket and the crane crunched crispy crackers by the creek. Answers will vary.
6. The speedy spider spun a sparkly web in space. Answers will vary.
7. The train traveled through traffic with a troop of trucks and tractors. Answers will vary.

Answers will vary.

page 24

1. screen; strike; scream; scold
2. straight; stray; sprout; splinter
3. spray; strong; scrape; squirm
4. split; spine; splash; streak
5. stream; scratch; straw; sprain
6. scrub; scrap; scoop; strain

str; str; scr; str; scr; str; spr; spl; str

page 25

screw; straw
sprain; street
splash; scrub

1. sprinkler

2. spring
3. scream
4. strawberry
5. scratch
6. strong
7. street

page 26
nt; mp; lt
nk; ft; mp

1. Mr. Flores is a scientist who works with a chi(mp) named Moe.
2. Mr. Flores is trying to learn how animals thi(nk).
3. Moe cannot talk, but Mr. Flores spe(nt) a long time teaching him sign language.
4. Whenever Mr. Flores fe(lt) that Moe earned a reward, he gave him a plu(mp) banana.
5. Moe learned to make signs for words like dr(in)k so(ft) sleep, wa(nt) and funny.
6. When Moe signs a word correctly, he ju(mp)s for joy.
7. "You're a cha(mp) Moe," cheers Mr. Flores.

page 27

1. Next weekend, we are going to ___ca(mp)___ at the Blue Spruce State Park. (camp, damp, colt)
2. We'll sleep in our new, three-room ___te(nt)___. (rent, tank, tent)
3. Dad said that we'll set up camp on a bed of ___so(ft)___ pine needles. (sift, soft, salt)
4. I can't wait to ___ra(ft)___ down Spruce River. (raft, rank, craft)
5. My sister, Linh, is worried the raft will ___si(nk)___. (wink, sent, sink)
6. My uncle ___le(nt)___ us some lifejackets, so now Linh is excited too. (lent, tint, lamp)
7. At night, we'll ___dr(in)k___ cocoa and roast marshmallows. (dunk, drink, drift)
8. I like my marshmallows ___bur(nt)___ to a crisp on the outside. (bent, shift, burnt)
9. Last night, I ___fe(lt)___ so excited I could hardly sleep. (felt, front, blink)
10. I just hope we don't get sprayed by a ___sku(nk)___ like my grandpa did the last time he went camping! (slump, skunk, trunk)

page 28
ld; nd; sk
st; sk; st
nd; st; ld

page 29

1. wri(st)	risk	_roast_	wild
2. di(sk)	build	send	_ask_
3. mo(ld)	_field_	blind	sound
4. sta(nd)	child	_grind_	post
5. ju(st)	task	_east_	sold
6. unfo(ld)	_held_	hound	twist
7. wo(nd)	trust	disk	_and_
8. ta(sk)	_ask_	wind	billfold

1. dentist
2. west
3. mask
4. band
5. blend
6. old
7. gold
8. disk
9. cold
10. toast

page 30

sku(nk)	sta(mp)	ne(st)
honk	dump	crust
a(nt)	be(lt)	ra(ft)
amount	salt	left

strawberry; split; screened;
stroll; street; strange;
sprang; splattered;
screamed; sprinted;
streamed; screens; scratch;
scraped

page 31
nd; ld; nd; nk; nd; st; st; nt;
nd; mp; ft; nd; st; lt; nd

page 32

(sh)eep — Answers will vary.
(ch)air — Answers will vary.
(ch)erry — Answers will vary.
(ch)eese — Answers will vary.
(sh)ovel — Answers will vary.
(sh)adow — Answers will vary.

1. sharp
2. shark
3. cheap
4. chin

page 33
1. child
2. shine
3. chip
4. choose
5. shower
6. shade

1. ch
2. sh
3. ch
4. sh
5. sh
6. ch
7. sh
8. ch
9. ch
10. sh

page 34

(th)umb — Answers will vary.
(ph)one — Answers will vary.
(wh)ale — Answers will vary.

Read each word in bold. Circle the digraph. Then, circle the word beside it that has the same beginning sound. If you are not sure, say the words out loud. Hint: The sounds can be the same even when the spellings are different. (Example: phase and fancy)

1. (th)irteen	them	_thief_	while
2. (th)at	third	phonics	_these_
3. (wh)at	thought	_wheat_	thanks
4. (ph)ew	_photo_	whip	poster
5. (th)irsty	those	phony	_thumb_
6. (wh)isk	throw	_water_	whose
7. (wh)om	when	_happy_	thick
8. (ph)ase	_fresh_	thimble	pink

page 35

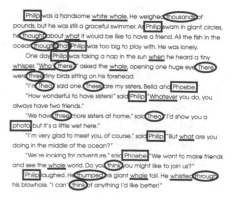

Philip was a handsome white whale. He weighed thousands of pounds, but he was still a graceful swimmer. As Philip swam in giant circles, he thought about what it would be like to have a friend. All the fish in the ocean thought that Philip was too big to play with. He was lonely.

One day Philip was taking a nap in the sun when he heard a tiny whisper. "Who's there?" asked the whale, opening one huge eye. There were three tiny birds sitting on his forehead.

"I'm Theo," said one. "These are my sisters, Bella and Phoebe."

"How wonderful to have sisters!" said Philip. "Whatever you do, you always have two friends."

"We have three more sisters at home," said Theo. "I'd show you a photo but it's a little wet here."

"I'm very glad to meet you, of course," said Philip. "But what are you doing in the middle of the ocean?"

"We're looking for adventure," said Phoebe. "We want to make friends and see the whole world. Do you think you might like to join us?"

Philip laughed. He thumped his giant whale tail. He whistled through his blowhole. "I can't think of anything I'd like better!"

Answer Key

page 36
1. watch
2. brush
3. photograph
4. lunch
5. north
6. leash
7. match
8. teeth

1. ch, Answers will vary
2. sh, Answers will vary
3. th, Answers will vary

page 37
th; ph; sh
ch; sh; th
th; ph; ch

page 38
duck; swing; laugh
wing; truck; sock

1. ng
2. gh
3. ck; ck
4. ng; gh
5. ng; ng; ng
6. ng; ng
7. ck; ck; ng

page 39
gh; ng; ng; ng; ng; ng; ck;
gh; ck, ck; ng; ck; ng; ng;
ng

ck
luck
track
clock
block

gh
tough
enough

ng
swimming
running
biking
long
training
belong
everything
finishing
anything

page 40
knot; wrinkle; knight

1. never
2. wrinkle
3. scissors
4. knob
5. seven
6. wrapper
7. nest
8. rail

page 41
1. writer
2. Knead
3. wrestling
4. scent
5. knows
6. scientist
7. knit
8. wreaths

1. wrong
2. scent
3. knight
4. scissors
5. wrap

page 42
hatchet; sleigh; pitcher
flashlight; stretch; thumb
hopscotch; lamb; night

comb; crutch; stoplight

page 43

1.	thumb	come	6.	comb	dome
2.	sleigh	way	7.	climb	dime
3.	limb	slim	8.	straight	hate
4.	flight	fright	9.	stitch	rich
5.	scratch	batch	10.	lamb	Sam

1. sketch
2. crumbs
3. sight
4. itches
5. might
6. sunlight
7. limb

page 44
1. thunder
2. thirteen
3. sandwich
4. sheep
5. king
6. black
7. laugh
8. phone

page 45
wr; sc; ng; sh; ck
ng; ph; gh; kn, wr, th
gh, ng, gh
ng, Wh

page 46
trash; tank; clam
fan; cab; math

1. Cass, and, Matt, tanks
2. plan, and, cash
3. Grant, Cass, and, Matt,
   bank, and
4. man, at, hand, and,
   Grants, catch
5. asked, batch, plants, and
6. back, at, Cass, and, Matt

7. Dan, Sam, and, Max, Grants, cats

page 47
bed; neck; shell
tent; dress; sled

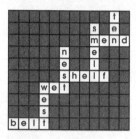

page 48
sick; bib; ship
cliff; grill; twins

1. Big
2. ringing
3. hitched
4. films
5. lit
6. still
7. wind

page 49
mop; knock; ox
frog; lock; pond

1. sock
2. hop
3. rock
4. top
5. blond

page 50
jump, fluff; sun, lunch; rug, junk; thumb, scrub; truck, mud; skunk, dust

1. drums
2. strums, hums

3. thumps, drummer's
4. puffs, trumpet
5. clutches, trusty
6. chugs, cup, punch
7. shuts, plugs

page 51

short a	short e	short i
has	them	kids
than	gets	things
that	tells	Civil
ask	check	ship
		visits
		trip

short o	short u
dogs	ducks
lots	up
got	mummy

page 52

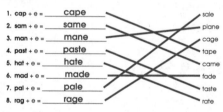

1. cap + e = cape
2. sam + e = same
3. man + e = mane
4. past + e = paste
5. hat + e = hate
6. mad + e = made
7. pal + e = pale
8. rag + e = rage

sale
plane
cage
tape
came
fade
taste
rate

1. wage
2. quake
3. vane
4. vase
5. cave
6. waste

page 53
1. mice, spice, white, rice.
2. dive, tide, spines, spikes, stripes
3. dine, nice, slice, lime, ripe, vine
4. wise, hike, nine, miles, rise
5. swine, glide, slide, slime, time, fine
6. Wipe, shine, side, pile,

twice
7. five, fine, kites, twine
8. bride, glide, five, miles, while, skydives

1–4. Answers will vary but should include long **i** words with the **i-consonant-e** spelling.

page 54
nose; rope; smoke
toe; globe; bone

1. doe
2. mole
3. Rome
4. joke
5. home
6. rose
7. whole

page 55
1. cube
2. rude
3. plume
4. tune
5. dude
6. cute
7. fuse

1. June; Sue
2. rule; due
3. tune; flute
4. cute; mule
5. clues

page 56
plate, Answers will vary.;
nine, Answers will vary.;
cone, Answers will vary.
glue, Answers will vary.;
dice, Answers will vary.;

cake, Answers will vary.
bike, Answers will vary.;
rose, Answers will vary.;
whale, Answers will vary.

page 57

long a
state
make
name
Lake

long i
shines
Pine
Line

long o
home
close
Lone
vote

long u
clue
blue

page 58
1. short
2. long
3. long
4. long
5. short
6. short
7. short
8. long
9. short
10. long
11. short
12. short

1. hot pot; short **o**
2. mad dad; short **a**
3. space place; long **a**
4. best nest; short **e**

5. cute flute; long **u**
6. twin grin; short **i**
7. whale sale; long **a**

page 59
long **i**; short **u**; long **o**;
short **u**; short **i**; shirt **e**;
short **a**; long **i**; short **a**;
long **i**; short **e**; short **u**;
short **a**; long **a**; short **i**;
long **i**; short **a**; long **a**

page 60
1. bait
2. neigh
3. day
4. Maine
5. veil
6. jay
7. snail
8. eight

page 61
trail; Rail; train; mail; freight;
remained; paid; laid;
Maine; straight; may; away;
day; reins

page 62
beak; bee; movie
wheel; thief; peach

tree	pea	shield
seed	treat	field
three	reach	collie
sneeze	sea	piece
creek	beat	niece
speech	plead	chief

page 63
1. ee
2. ea
3. ie

4. ea
5. ee
6. ee
7. ee
8. ie
9. ea
10. ea
11. ea
12. ea; ea
13. ee

page 64
1. tight
2. thigh
3. wild
4. midnight
5. blind
6. kind
7. child
8. behind
9. flashlight
10. mind

page 65
1. child
2. right
3. wind
4. light
5. find
6. high
7. midnight
8. wild

1. sing
2. whip
3. sling
4. trip
5. flip
6. chin
7. bit
8. hint

page 66
cold; toast; snow

1. road
2. Coach
3. gold
4. most
5. known
6. goal

page 67

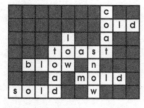

1. most
2. foam
3. row
4. scold
5. coast
6. mow

page 68
beach; peach
goat; float
thigh; sigh
hay; tray
knee; three
cold; bold
tail; rail
snow; glow
eight; weight

1. sail
2. bay
3. rip
4. flap

page 69
long **e** as in pea: sea;
weak; leaves; teach

long **e** as in beep:
seen; deep; keeps; feels;
need
long **e** as in chief: piece;
fields
long **i** as in night: knight;
upright
long **i** as in child: wild
long **a** as in day: sway; stay

page 70
moose; Answers will vary.
screw; Answers will vary.
hook; Answers will vary.

good; books; few;
cartoons; Pooh; kangaroo;
gloomy; crew; grew;
school; too; knew

page 71
1. chew   stew
2. zoo   drool
3. spoon   flew
4. stood   brook
5. hoot   dew
6. gloom   loop
7. foot   hood
8. goose   snooze

moon; moon; looks; moons;
moon; loom; moon; took;
good; knew; moon; moons;
too; moons; new; moon;
Moon; Moon; Moon; Moon;
Moon;

page 72
1. bawl
2. law
3. caught
4. dawn
5. slaw

6. launch
7. gnaw
8. raw

1. crawl
2. lawn
3. author
4. yawn
5. August
6. paw
7. auto
8. saw
9. fawn
10. straw

page 73
aw   au   aw
aw   aw   au

1. launch
2. author
3. taught
4. because
5. jigsaw
6. sausage

page 74
1. oy
2. oy
3. oy
4. oy
5. oi
6. oi

1. Roy, Troy, McCoy,
   cowboys
2. annoy, loyal
3. Roy, joined, voyage
4. Troy, enjoys, coiled
5. Troy, Roy, pointing, noise
6. McCoy, broiled
7. boiled, sirloin, foil,
   cowboys

Answer Key

page 75

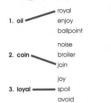

1. oil — royal, enjoy, ballpoint
2. coin — noise, broiler, join
3. loyal — joy, spoil, avoid
4. soy — soil, choice, boy
5. joint — point, moist, foil
6. choice — poison, voice, tinfoil

1. soy
2. coins
3. loyal
4. voice
5. noise
6. spoil
7. point
8. joined

page 76
cloud, proud; clown, brown; house, blouse

1. Brown
2. proud
3. cloud
4. hound
5. doghouse
6. ground

page 77
1. grouch
2. howl
3. flour
4. frown
5. pound
6. sour
7. plow

1. trout
2. scowl
3. pouch
4. gown
5. hour
6. town
7. growl

page 78
1. a cozy place for reading — mouse house
2. a dog that eats too much — stew crew
3. a fun place to swim — loose goose
4. a group of people who make soup — round hound
5. the nose of a fish — book nook
6. a trusty queen — trout snout
7. a home for a rodent — cool pool
8. a bird that got away — loyal royal

1. straw
2. coins
3. pounce
4. flew
5. stood

page 79

spoon	saw	cow
flew	lawn	bounce
boot	caught	gown
brew	sauce	prowl
zoo	draw	hour

hawk, found, caught, join, good, food, enjoy, schools, owl, without

page 80
1. long **e**
2. long **i**
3. long **e**
4. **y**
5. long **i**
6. long **e**
7. **y**

1. forty
2. dry
3. jelly
4. young
5. penny
6. yellow

page 81

long i	long e	y
Tyler	only	yo-yo
try	party	years

fly
city
tricky
easy
country
exactly
lately
baby

shiny
yank
yet
young

page 82

bird   nurse   circle
turtle   skirt   letter

1. e
2. i
3. a
4. f
5. b
6. j
7. c
8. d
9. g
10. h

page 83
1. er
2. ir; er
3. er; er
4. ur
5. ur; er
6. ur
7. ir; ir
8. er; er

1. **herd**, shirt
2. **perk**, under
3. **purse**, girl
4. **birthday**, fern
5. **curve**, chirp
6. **dirty**, person

page 84

corn	shark
thorn	arch
sport	cart
porch	scar
cord	tart

1. large
2. garden
3. fork
4. yarn
5. snore
6. north

page 85

farmers'; morning; farms; markets; stores; far; charged; for; large; corn; more; pork; Organic; arts; garden; cart; start; larger

page 86
1. scarf
2. spy
3. after
4. horse
5. family
6. yam
7. jar
8. letter
9. yolk
10. turtle

page 87

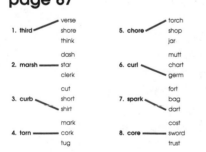

1. dry, fry, my, long **i**

2. baby, bunny, lucky, pretty, long **e**
3. Yesterday, Yoko, yelled, yellow, **y**
4. fly, sky, long **i**

page 88

Base Word	Add ed	Add ing
chop	chopped	chopping
hike	hiked	hiking
bloom	bloomed	blooming
plan	planned	planning
spy	spied	spying
hope	hoped	hoping
hum	hummed	humming
carry	carried	carrying
suggest	suggested	suggesting
clap	clapped	clapping
try	tried	trying
act	acted	acting
hug	hugged	hugging

page 89

located; moving; interviewed; allowed; examined; passed; traveling; cried; starting; seeing; stopped

1. study
2. quiz
3. live
4. marry

(page 90)
1. barks
2. coaxes
3. studies
4. rings
5. latches
6. kisses
7. empties
8. waxes

(page 91)
1. tosses
2. rushes
3. tries, crashes

4. calls, watches
5. wags, brings
6. kisses, gives
7. hurries, buries

1. mix
2. fry
3. talk
4. crunch
5. marry
6. brush
7. clap
8. cry
9. hiss
10. dance
11. wash
12. bake

(page 92)
1. hottest
2. driest
3. wettest
4. wetter
5. sunnier
6. coldest

(page 93)

Base Word	Add er	Add est
safe	safer	safest
thin	thinner	thinnest
sweet	sweeter	sweetest
warm	warmer	warmest
strange	stranger	strangest
busy	busier	busiest

1. friendliest
2. quieter
3. largest
4. gentler
5. fluffiest
6. thinner
7. smarter

I blend: Blossom; Blaze; fluffiest

Answer Key

r blend: Brady; friendliest; friendlier; Bridget; brothers; bright

page 94

Base Word	Add s or es	Add ed	Add ing
watch	watches	watched	watching
taste	tastes	tasted	tasting
finish	finishes	finished	finishing
skip	skips	skipped	skipping
miss	misses	missed	missing
relax	relaxes	relaxed	relaxing
laugh	laughs	laughed	laughing
try	tries	tried	trying
jump	jumps	jumped	jumping
explore	explores	explored	exploring
fuss	fusses	fussed	fussing
drip	drips	dripped	dripping
worry	worries	worried	worrying

page 95
1. smaller
   Answers will vary.
2. strangest
   Answers will vary.
3. funniest
   Answers will vary.
4. biggest
   Answers will vary.

liked; bigger; working; gentlest; braver; quitting; talking; making; founded; pleased; touches

page 96
cherry; cherries
dress; dresses
wheel; wheels
ball; balls
baby; babies
knife; knives

1. families
2. coaches
3. teammates
4. bases

page 97
1. party
2. thief
3. spoon
4. pony
5. peach
6. dolphin
7. class
8. diary
9. leaf

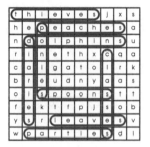

page 98
1. children
2. sheep
3. women
4. moose
6. geese

1. sheep
2. geese
3. mouse; mice
4. men

page 99
1. moose; S
2. trout; P
3. children; P
4. feet; P
5. series; S
6. die; S
   dice; P

1. b
2. a
3. a

4. b

page 100
1. Will's homework
2. the squirrel's tale
3. the computer's keyboard
4. the school's gym
5. Charles's eyes
6. the movie's actors
7. the library's books
8. Malika's smile
9. the dress's colors

1. PL
2. PO
3. PL
4. PO
5. PO

page 101
1. the campers' tents
2. the boys' sleeping bags
3. the campfires' flames
4. the crickets' chirping
5. the children's singing
6. the backpacks' zippers
7. the flashlights' beams
8. the food's smells

chirping   children   flashlights
crickets   backpacks

page 102
1. SP
2. PP
3. PL
4. SP
5. PP
6. PP
7. PL
8. SP

Answer Key

1. a
2. b
3. a
4. a

canary, cats', cage
guinea
gerbils

page 103
1. The sisters' teacher is Mrs. Huong.
2. The bus's schedule is posted on the bulletin board.
3. The lyrics are on the inside of the CD's case.
4. Antoine's friend will be here at noon.
5. The game's pieces are still inside the box.
6. The butterflies' wings seem to shimmer in the sunlight.
7. Be careful not to let go of the balloons' strings.
8. The painting's frame is cracked.
9. The skaters' jackets were warm and cozy.
10. The alarm clock's ring is loud and shrill.

page 104

Singular	Plural	Singular Possessive	Plural Possessive
book	books	book's	books'
woman	women	woman's	women's
wolf	wolves	wolf's	wolves'
egg	eggs	egg's	eggs'
library	libraries	library's	libraries'
sheep	sheep	sheep's	sheep's
mouse	mice	mouse's	mice's
dish	dishes	dish's	dishes'
city	cities	city's	cities'

1. schools; Answers will vary.
2. buses; Answers will vary.
3. leaves; Answers will vary.
4. beaches; Answers will vary.
5. countries; Answers will vary.
6. computers; Answers will vary.
7. stories; Answers will vary.
8. foxes; Answers will vary.

page 105
PL; SP; PL; PP; PL, SP

1. Muir's
2. grizzlies
3. tribes
4. trees'
5. species
6. Grasses
7. Hikers
8. families
9. deer
10. wolves
11. rangers'

page 106
1. fingernail
2. popcorn
3. starfish
4. doorbell
5. football
6. horseback
7. sunflower
8. wheelchair

1. note, book
2. back, yard
3. sand, box
4. snow, ball
5. tea, spoon
6. news, paper

page 107
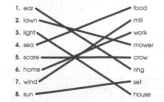
1. lunchroom
2. pinecone
3. nightgown
4. washcloth
5. newspaper
6. sailboat
7. spaceship

page 108
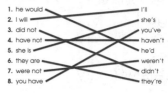
1. hasn't
2. She's
3. wasn't
4. He'll
5. shouldn't
6. That's

page 109
1. are
2. will
3. I'm
4. would/had
5. she's
6. is/has
7. could
8. I've
9. are
10. he

1. don't; do not
2. doesn't; does not
3. they'd; they would

4. can't; can not
5. What's; What is

page 110
1. I'm
2. He'll
3. haven't
4. they're
5. We've
6. It's
7. won't

1. Who is; Who's
2. We will; We'll
3. can not; can't
4. has not; hasn't
5. She has; She's
6. would not; wouldn't

page 111
1. they have; **ha**
2. what is; **i**
3. we are; **a**
4. did not; **o**
5. let us; **u**
6. that is; **i**
7. I am; **a**
8. should not; **o**
9. she will; **wi**
10. would have; **ha**

1. shouldn't
2. We're
3. I've
4. won't
5. Don't
6. could've

th; wh; sh

page 112
cupcake; bedroom;
motorcycle; anteater;

rainbow; backpack;
waterfall; teacup; airplane

1. backseat; backyard;
   backbone
2. birdbath; birdcage;
   birdseed
3. fireworks; firefly; fireplace;
   firestorm
4. sunshine; sunburn;
   sunrise; sunbath
5. snowflake; snowstorm
6. toothbrush; toothpaste

page 113

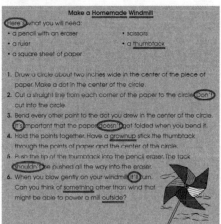

page 114
1. unable; not able
2. disagree; not agree
3. dislike; not like
4. unsure; not sure
5. unequal; not equal
6. distrust; not trust

1. unpack; Answers will vary.
2. disappear; Answers will
   vary.
3. unplug; Answers will vary.
4. disobey; Answers will
   vary.

page 115

1. impolite — not polite
2. incorrect — not correct
3. invisible — not visible
4. impatient — not patient
5. inexpensive — not expensive
6. impossible — not possible
7. incomplete — not complete
8. inexact — not exact

1. indirect
2. impolite
3. impure
4. incorrect
5. indoors
6. impossible

page 116
1. preorder
2. repack
3. misread
4. prewash
5. recheck
6. premix
7. misjudge

1. recount; to count again
2. predawn; before dawn
3. misconnect; connect
   badly
4. precook; cook before
5. resell; to sell again
6. misname; to name
   wrongly

page 117
1. overcharge
2. underweight
3. underdress
4. overcook
5. underrate
6. oversize

1. underwater
2. overrated
3. underline
4. overthink

5. overslept
6. underground

page 118
1. messy; Answers will vary.
2. quickly; Answers will vary.
3. bouncy; Answers will vary.
4. softly; Answers will vary.
5. easily; Answers will vary.
6. lucky; Answers will vary.

1. strongly
2. rusty
3. safely
4. tricky
5. steamy
6. noisily

page 119
1. teacher
2. painter
3. sailor
4. inventor
5. farmer
6. governor

1. a person who sculpts
2. a person who collects
3. a person who gardens
4. a person who builds
5. a person who runs

page 120

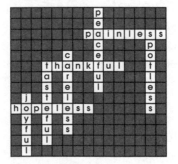

page 121
1. bendable
2. breakable
3. hidden
4. strengthen
5. broken

1. harden; to make hard
2. lovable; able to be loved
3. washable; able to be washed
4. widen; to make wider
5. sharpen; to make sharp

page 122
1. e
2. a
3. b
4. f
5. c
6. d

1. unafraid
2. rethought
3. prearranged
4. overload
5. unsure
6. mislead

page 123
1. actor; Answers will vary.
2. stormy; Answers will vary.
3. beautiful; Answers will vary.
4. valuable; Answers will vary.

1. sleepily
2. endless
3. darken
4. fixable
5. leader

page 124
balloon, 2; tree, 1;
kangaroo, 3
pretzel, 2; bicycle, 3;
monkey, 2

1. Which two picture names have the vowel sound you hear in goose?
   balloon   kangaroo
2. Which two picture names begin with a two-letter blend? Circle the blend.
   (tr)ee   (pr)etzel

page 125
1. air/plane
2. dis/like
3. pic/ture
4. cook/book
5. re/fill
6. bath/tub
7. bee/hive
8. pre/heat
9. lum/ber
10. un/do

1. Mon/day, den/tist, tooth/ache
2. win/ter, foot/prints, side/walk
3. sun/light, in/doors
4. Wel/come, some/one
5. un/tied, hall/way
6. dis/like, of/fice

page 126
1 syllable	2 syllables
wind	sea/shore
bench	un/lock
shrimp	ta/ble
fish	lad/der
star	si/lent
breeze	home/sick

3 syllables
cu/cum/ber
won/der/ful

Answer Key

pop/u/lar
ter/ri/ble
ad/ven/ture
el/e/phant

1. mitten
2. vacation
3. sled
4. before
5. factory
6. pinch
7. paper
8. hammer
9. loose

page 127
1. Hurricane, Katrina
2. Many, people, around, wanted
3. Maryland, difference
4. started, Project, Backpack
5. Jackie, Jenna, Kantor, backpacks, along
6. They, reached, their, goal, of
7. around, country, about, project
8. They, in, their, own, too
9. areas, Katrina
10. Even, Kantor, sisters, only, thousands, never, even

1. many
2. Coast
3. goal

page 128
wink, 1; mailbox, 2; banana, 3; mosquito, 3; snowflake, 2; pear, 1

2; 2

1; 1
2; 2
2; 2
3; 3
2; 2
3; 3
1; 1
2; 2
2; 2

page 129
1. puzzle; insect
2. snake; rug
3. pumpkin; notebook
4. fish; bowl
5. butterfly; forever

cac/tus; most/ly; ar/e/as;
con/di/tions; Un/like;
In/stead; pro/tect; des/ert;
an/i/mals; wa/ter; flesh/y;
in/to; o/ther; o/ver; wi/der
a/bout; spe/cies;
South/west; Mex/i/co

page 130
pail; smile; present
rabbit; hat; rip

1. terrific
2. sleepy
3. giant
4. destroy
5. giggle

page 131
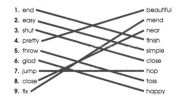

1. pick
2. tug
3. quiet
4. stop
5. broke
6. scream
7. small
8. see
9. keep

page 132
1. bottom
2. white
3. friend
4. morning
5. down
6. hate
7. under

1. white
2. friend

page 133
short; bad; easy; smaller; weaker; slower; woman; less; finished; lost; fake; boring

page 134
1. A
2. S
3. S
4. A
5. S
6. A
7. A

8. S
9. S
10. A
11. S
12. A

1. messy
2. full
3. lost
4. ill
5. wrong
6. infant
7. west
8. noisy
9. find
10. smooth

page 135
1. largest
2. country
3. new
4. makes
5. easier
6. grows
7. autumn
8. first
9. long
10. lost

page 136
bear; shoe; eye
eight; pear; sun
night; flower; ant

eight   night   knight

page 137
1. Answers will vary but should include the correct use of cent.
2. Answers will vary but should include the correct use of close.

3. Answers will vary but should include the correct use of meat.
4. Answers will vary but should include the correct use of hear.

1. bye; buy
2. four; for
3. high; hi
4. road; rode
5. they're; there

page 138
1. Answers will vary. Possible answer: A fly is sitting on the picnic table.
2. Answers will vary. Possible answer: Casey is up to bat next.
3. Answers will vary. Possible answer: Daisy has a loud bark.
4. Answers will vary. Possible answer: What is today's date?
5. Answers will vary. Possible answer: The bikes are in the yard.
6. Answers will vary. Possible answer: Strawberry jam is my favorite.
7. Answers will vary. Possible answer: That pen leaked ink on my shirt!
8. Answers will vary. Possible answer: Tell me a story, Mom.

page 139
1. b
2. a
3. a

4. b
5. a
6. b
7. b
8. a

1. Which two words have the long i sound?
fine   kind
2. Which two words have a silent consonant? Circle the consonant.
pitcher   watch

page 140
1. S
2. M
3. M
4. M
5. S
6. S
7. M
8. S

1. Answers will vary. Possible answer: a cat's.
2. Answers will vary. Possible answer: a hundred bees.
3. Answers will vary. Possible answer: honey.
4. Answers will vary. Possible answer: marbles.

page 141
Fiona and Nora walked down the sandy path to the beach. It was the middle of the day, and the sand felt like hot coals under their bare feet. They walked faster, trying not to let their feet touch the sand for long. The water was a blue carpet stretching out toward the sky. It looked cool and inviting from the hot beach.

"It's beautiful here, isn't it?" said Nora. She turned her face to the sun that hung like a fat, yellow grapefruit in the sky. Nora sniffed the salty breeze. "The ocean air smells as fresh as clean laundry."

The girls found their parents and spread out their towels. They were careful not to wake their dad, who slept like a baby under a large umbrella. Suddenly, Fiona spotted a pelican. It was a missile zooming toward the water. A moment later, it flew away with a wriggling fish sticking out of its beak. "There's always something going on at the beach!" laughed Fiona.

1. house; dinosaur
2. stomachs; bottomless pits
3. Marcus's legs; rubber

Answer Key

page 142
hair; horse; bee
deer; ring; muscle

1. sale
2. Meet, hour
3. peak
4. Your

Answers will vary. Possible answers shown.
1. Dad chopped some wood for the fire.
   Would you like to go to my softball game?
2. There is only one apple left.
   Quinn won the first game of checkers.
3. I like my pizza plain.
   The plane landed two hours late.

page 143
1. A tear rolled down the girl's cheek.
2. The seal has thick, gray fur.
3. Rest quietly until lunch.
4. We never use the old well in the yard.
5. What's inside the box?

1. S; rain, tiny footsteps
2. M; Britta, apple of my eye
3. M; snow, a thick, white blanket
4. S; heavy meal, a rock
5. S; children, mice

tiny; proudly; heavy

page 144
1. 2, 3, 1
2. 2, 1, 3
3. 1, 3, 2
4. 1, 3, 2
5. 3, 2, 1
6. 2, 3, 1

1. hers, line, mile, minnow
2. skunk, sled, sleigh, sloth
3. net, news, nibble, niece

1. phase
2. sloth, sleigh, sled

page 145
Bloomers!
Coming on Home Soon
High as a Hawk
The House of Wisdom
Piggins
Squids Will Be Squids
Superfudge

page 146
1. fork
2. dice
3. pink
4. herself
5. wing

1–4. Answers will vary.

forgave, format, forty, fork, hickory

page 147
ball * bandage
ballet
balloon
bamboo
band
balmy

bark * bath
base
barrel
barn
batch
basket

1. 220
2. 84
3. 85
4. 222
5. 85
6. 220
7. 84
8. 222
9. 85
10. 222
11. 220
12. 85
13. 84
14. 222
15. 220
16. 84
17. 85
18. 222

bit * blaze
blame
black
blade
blanket
blast

page 148
1. lesson
2. hide
3. activity
4. wrap
5. scold
6. hungry
7. fox
8. trip
9. carry
10. laugh
11. thin
12. wash

1. 2
2. no
3. 2

page 149
enjoy; record; book; adult;
publish; children; call;
folktale; write; write; kid;
story; tale; tiger; spot

born; recorded

page 150
Babbitt, Natalie
Banks, Lynne Reid
Byars, Betsy
Christopher, Matt
Cleary, Beverly
Dahl, Roald
Lasky, Kathryn
Lowry, Lois
Pinkney, Jerry
Wallace, Bill
White, E. B.

1. glasses; glad • globe
2. flower; floppy • flute
3. spoon; sponge • sprout

page 151
1. spaniel, sparkle, story
2. stories
3. sparkle
4. story
5. sparkle
6. 1

1. rag, rain, recycle, reflect
2. beach, cry, fling, slide
3. fan, fast, father, feast
4. invite, island, ladybug,
   lamp